'I love pop music. It is the only branch of the humanities which evokes such a bizarre and overwhelming response. One doesn't ever see a chart of the best paintings and then thousands of people flocking to the gallery to scream hysterically at the piece voted number one, even when it makes no sense whatsoever.'

D. Philpott, Magazine Interview

'I am not for a second suggesting that art be subject to regulation or trading standards but we as the consumer and audience are surely perfectly entitled to ask questions of the creator? I do get the wrong end of the stick though sometimes.'

D. Philpott, Café Spike Interview

'Dear 'The Clash': You state that if you go there will be trouble and if you stay it will be double. Therefore, I would advise you to go, as this would minimise any potential 'trouble'. Have you perhaps fallen foul of the new parking restrictions on Overcliff Drive in Bournemouth?'

W. Turnbull, 2010

INTRODUCTION

In 2008, I was at a wedding with my friend Wilf Turnbull – who, like myself, is a retired gentleman from Bournemouth – when the DJ played, as Wilf put it, 'those Jacksons'. I admit that, at this juncture, ale had been copiously imbibed at the free bar and after a third mushroom vol-au-vent, as little Michael and the rest of his sibling quintet's song filled the air (not literally), I remember Wilf suddenly standing stock-still and declaring that sunshine, moonlight, good times and boogie can hardly be held accountable for a failed romance. Then, as I was mid-chicken drumstick, the DJ put on Living In A Box and we wondered why in heaven's name a pop star would be residing within a cardboard box, given that the job is notoriously well paid?

I asked Wilf what in the blazes we were going to do about it, and after a bit of thought, we decided that there was only one course of action available to us: we would write to both of them, and take them to task over their questionable lyrics.

We very soon realised that The Jacksons and Living In A Box were by no means the only pop culprits guilty of lyrical ambiguities and inaccuracies. As our journey through decades of pop and rock began, we discovered more and more dubious claims and declarations which we felt needed to be addressed and clarified as a matter of urgency. We were polite yet firm – sometimes merely proffering advice – and from time to time we apparently got the wrong end of the stick, but we carried on regardless. Sometimes we invited artists to events in our home town of Bournemouth (a place we referenced frequently); they are just normal people after all… aren't they?

The scope and reach of our letters expanded when some younger family members, who are extremely knowledgeable in musical matters, caught wind of our exploits and proceeded to expose us to pop groups and music that we wouldn't otherwise have chanced upon. I would sometimes wonder if the young scamps weren't baiting us when, after playing us some 'offending material', they would chuckle and ask:

'Are they human or are they dancer?? Are you REALLY going to let them get away with that??!!'

We were not quite sure where this was taking us, but knew we wanted to share the fruits of our labours. So, with encouragement and help from the young mischief makers (and some admittedly bemused friends), social networking pages were created for us, and a wonderful website with links to all our letters was built by the brilliant James Marett at Oast One. I cannot thank James enough for both his initial brilliance and then incredible patience and politeness over the years, during which I once phoned him at 10 o'clock GMT to ask why all the letters had vanished when the site was merely undergoing maintenance. He was on a ski slope, but he didn't shout.

From the very humble beginnings of chatting amongst ourselves to fifty or so 'virtual friends', the interest in our letters began to grow organically and swiftly. We remain close friends, and I am honoured and delighted that he still helps out when able (superbly, I may add), but at this time Wilf decided to take a back seat simply because of other commitments. My own output became so prolific that he felt I was handling pop lyric affairs more than amply by myself.

The popularity of the letters began to climb exponentially, and rumours even spread that they were the work not of 'Joe Public', but of music journalists and people connected to the upper echelons of the business – even the artists themselves! Questions were raised in Parliament*.

* Not really.

Then, one day in 2010, the most remarkable and quite unexpected thing happened… *the pop stars began to reply!*

I can take no personal credit for this remarkable development. Although I had tentatively sent the letters to the artists via 'official channels' (i.e. management and record companies), my requests for responses, perhaps understandably, fell on deaf ears. Quite simply, as my online status grew to astonishing levels, it was my army of 'fans' and friends of all ages, from all over the world, who have been wholly instrumental in putting me in touch with an ever-growing number of musicians, either through personal associations or their standings as long-term fans of the artists. My 'good-natured haranguing notoriety' escalated at an alarming rate. Eventually, I even achieved the point whereby the pop stars, management and agents *et cetera* were discussing my exploits and feeding me 'leads' (via the back door of the industry, so to speak). Some were even *requesting* that I write to them.

So here I am, featured in the mainstream media; on hundreds of internet forums and websites; on the radio and in magazines worldwide; and being invited backstage to 'hang out' with pop stars who, I am flattered to say, love the letters and enjoy getting involved via their responses. Indeed, I am very pleased to have acted, in my own small way, as a conduit between the pop stars and their followers; the latter who often gleefully get in touch to thank me for finally getting to the bottom of a lyrical conundrum that had been bugging them for years, and the former pleased to respond via a friendly and light-hearted public platform to answer questions that are often asked of them.

I have had many approaches over the years to compile my letters into a book. Having investigated all possibilities, I eventually decided that by far the best method of doing so was to do it myself, via the crowdfunding route. Some publishers in the distant past have insisted that some letters be 'toned down' – tweaked, or a certain long or flowery word omitted as 'no one knows what that means' – which I found unacceptable. By 'going it alone', not only do I retain full creative control, but, just as crucially, this wonderful organic process, nurtured to fruition by family, friends and fans from social media sites, together with many other supporters both at home and abroad, continues.

So, friends old and new, thank you, thank you all for this wonderful and completely unexpected journey at this juncture in my life. It's been – and continues to be – emotional.

I have to go now. Bargain Hunt's on.

PS Obviously a lot of the time the artists do *not* reply or I am unable to connect with them, which is perfectly reasonable. The 'mini letters' I post to my internet friends, related to these unanswered ramblings (and my random thoughts) have also proved popular and many of these are included here too. :)

PHILPOTTERY

Scattered throughout the following pages you will find pictures of, amongst others, 'Lady BudgeriGaGa', 'The Snoutorious P.I.G.' and 'Nine Inch Snails'.

My letters can take hours to construct, so a couple of years ago, rather than sitting next to me doing nothing, my wife Jean took to making plasticine pop star animals, incorporating the trademark features of certain artists into her creations. The reaction on social media was so incredible – with people actually asking to buy her artistry – that we invested in professional modelling clay and tools and now make fridge magnets and wall plaques for people. They either pick from those already 'out there' in 'cyberspace', give us their own wonderful suggestions, or select from the wonderful suggestions of others. They are completely and individually handmade from blocks of clay; no templates, moulds, cutouts or other (if you pardon the pun) 'shortcuts' are used in the crafting process. Jean has now honed her skills to such an extent that she is able to sculpt pets and family members from personal photographs. Very much like the letters, this genuine cottage industry started from nothing and, thanks to our 'virtual friends', has erupted and continues to evolve. We now have customers all over the world.

For more information we'd be delighted if you visited www.facebook.com/philpottery

THE LETTERS

Dear Rick Wakeman,

As a fellow parent, I hope that you can be of assistance.

Regretfully I must confide that my grandson's school has been lagging behind somewhat in the department of GCSE pass grades, according to the official Ofsted statistics. Upon close scrutiny of said cavillous data, a vast chasm of success between certain subjects included in the field of the humanities was unveiled. In order to rectify this situation it has been decided that the secondary modern should meld an area in which they excel with one that requires improvement, in order to perhaps subliminally spur the deficient pupils into favourable academia. They will therefore be staging a special event going for the one area of the curriculum that the students are most adept at, music, and combining it with history, where they are clearly floundering. This unique affair will be billed and promoted as 'Pastonbury'.

As the original artists have not as yet come back to us we have implemented a contingency plan by putting down 10% refundable deposits on tribute artists Phony M (Rasputin), NO.M.D. (Joan of Arc and possibly Enola Gay) and West London's foremost piano/vocal 'soundalike' Feltham John, who will be performing Candle In The Wind twice (covering off Marilyn Monroe and Princess Diana for no additional fee), before travelling back in time for a pre-booked engagement at Isleworth Royal British Legion.

We wonder if you would be willing to help out by coming along in the afternoon and doing your King Arthur after the tombola. As the event is pencilled in for mid-May there is unfortunately little chance of the playground freezing over in deference to The Empire Pool recitals, so we would be having you indoors, although you should be put on notice that the parquet flooring, not unlike the aforementioned auditorium's performance surface, can be particularly treacherous when newly waxed, especially when negotiated in socks.

One of the Heads of Year, Ms Braithwaite, who is a keen enthusiast of 'progressive rock', mooted that as you would be here anyway you may as well play The Six Wives of Henry VIII in its entirety. However, although she was thanked for her proactive suggestion, which was duly minuted, the Board of Governors voted to the contrary on the grounds that sadly they only had use of the Main Hall until 8pm, at which time it would have to be vacated in order to make way for the caretaker, and also that, being an instrumental piece, the children may become fidgety if sat cross-legged for such a long period. Furthermore, the organisers had not the resources to stage a slide show or 'PowerPoint presentation' with the facility to depict an image of each ecclesiastical revisionist spouse in order to distinguish one set of your 'moog stylings' and going up and down the keyboard as fast as possible from another. It was therefore instead decided that they would 'go with' the remnants of Herman's Hermits as a far less convoluted if admittedly factually inaccurate reference to said morbidly rotund tyrannical Tudor patriarch.

As they are somewhat restricted in terms of budget, it has been proposed that your fuel costs to and from Bournemouth would be fully reimbursed upon provision of valid receipts, and in order to save your back you will not be expected to bring your 'banks' of synthesisers, 'mellowtrons', electrical harpsichords and other such paraphernalia. You will instead be provided with two nearly new Bontempi organs temporarily borrowed by the gym mistress, Miss Mallard, from the stockroom of the local Sue Ryder shop on Wimbourne Road where she volunteers two hours of her time of a Saturday. This is an additional bonus for the co-ordinators as stage space is at a premium (although thankfully not vertically, given that the vaulted ceiling would provide ample room for your pointy hat).

Sadly, Mr Balakrishnan, whose daughter Neeta often brings authentic homemade dishes into school to share amongst her classmates and tutors, will not be in attendance as he will be away visiting relatives in Tamil Nadu. He would have been delighted to have provided you with bindi bhaji, stuffed paratha and Bombay aloo (of a fashion familiar to those inadvertently ordered by yourself on the Tales From Topographic Oceans tour and consumed during a lengthy 'percussive interlude'), but as a compromise we will be happy to send the school captain out to go and get a 60 piece Indian platter from the Iceland on Christchurch Road, which will be balanced 'close to the edge' of the instruments during your recital.

My wife, Jean, is something of a wizard seamstress and, as a token of thanks for your time, has acquiesced to run up a cape to add to your probably already varied and vast wardrobe, free of charge. The kaleido-scopic dolman would be adapted from last term's Year 10 production of Joseph and his Amazing Technicolour Dreamcoat's backdrop, and she has asked me to enquire after your collar and chest measurements, as well as your height, so that she can ensure a perfect fit.

We anxiously await your response, sir, and sincerely hope that it is one of acceptance, in order that we may not be forced to resort to Dick Fakeman.

Yours,

Derek Philpott

....

Dear Mr Philpott,

I am writing in regard to your kind invitation of the 18th March 2014, whereby you enquire of the possibility of my performing a mixed repertoire at your grandson's educational establishment. I was immediately drawn to the notion of the pupils' favouring both music and history and could not help but draw the conclusion that they must surely represent my next tier of fandom. One must there-fore take such requests with due sincerity and dignity.

I fear, however, that perhaps you are underestimating the workload therein, so feel duly obliged to appraise you of the undertaking.

Firstly, to the matter of King Arthur. Whilst I do note your scheduling and the likely, but not impossible, lack of ice, I should draw your attention to our backup plan of having the performers wear roller skates in lieu of ice skates. Surely the newly waxed auditorium would not fare well with the oft performed braking manoeuvres of the skaters, all performed, of course, in perfect synchronicity with the music? I fear I must insist on a disclaimer totally freeing the performers from any requirement to 'make good' the surface after the event.

And the horses? Perhaps the school has a gardening patch that could be used for the disposal of, well let's just say any aftermath of the horses' excitement at the Moog solos?

Moving on to the Six Wives, I do note your time reservations, but I perhaps should draw your attention to one of my lesser known works which was in fact the 4 Wives of Rick Wakeman, a recording in four movements but the first three of these are rarely played due to the expense necessary to relive these pieces of my history. The 4th movement is playable but is still ongoing and we have yet to reach the ending.

As to your kind reimbursement of petrol offer, I really think that given the somewhat charitable nature of this event, I could see my way to waiving those charges, especially now that modern orchestras are more than familiar with public transport – most bus doors these days being more than wide enough to accommodate the double bass and timpani that alas were ruled out by Routemasters – and most of the musicians I work with have bus passes.

And I fear you haven't read my riders of late. Whilst Mr Balakrishnan's cuisine would indeed have more than accommodated my needs in times gone by, you'll find me much slimmer these days. Perhaps the school captain could be persuaded to pick some choice salad greens, with perhaps a small request for radish? I certainly like to replace the curry effects where possible. These days most of my cuisine is in fact pureed.

Finally, the tipping point of the request must surely be the temptation of yet another cape for my collection; you just cannot have too many and they do tend to get somewhat tarnished and torn on the aforementioned public transport and also during my moonlighting exploits by helping out Batman when he's a bit busy. And to have it fashioned out of none other than a Technicolour Dreamcoat? Well, you obviously know my connections to dear Sir Tim Rice – a more fitting repurposing I cannot possibly imagine! I shall have my tailor forward current measurements forthwith (as previously noted, they're shrinking by the week!).

So in conclusion, Mr Philpott, I'm sure we can come to some arrangement for this performance. Whilst noting your standby of Mr Fakeman, I really don't want to leave you with a replacement Dick on the night. Replacement Dicks are so often a letdown.

I look forward to hearing more from you in due course...

With deep anticipation I await your reply,

Rick Wakeman

Dear Slade,

It was all I could do last week to stop myself from getting on the train to Wolverhampton and giving you all a good clip around the ear, knocking your ridiculous mirrored top hats off in the process.

For three glorious school terms, next door but one neighbour Gordon's grandson was the proud, if you will pardon the pun, 'holder' of his year's spelling trophy, and his lexical deftness and accuracy under tournament conditions made him the Bishop of Winchester Scrabble Club Champion. There was even talk of this linguistic prodigy ultimately being groomed for district championships as a springboard to Countdown.

Pandemonium, however, ensued in the assembly hall when he answered a routine preliminary challenge as 'P.L.E.E.Z.E.'. On a very icy (as in socially awkward as opposed to a frozen road surface) drive home from the tournament the disgraced young man admitted that his blunder was down to an overexposure to the printed track listing of your 'Sladest' hits compendium, which I have now read with repugnance. One may sadly remark, 'Look Wot You Dun', Slade. Your litany of orthographic shame does not, I regret, end here. Coz I Luv You, Take Me Bak 'Ome, Mama Weer All Crazee Now, Cum On Feel The Noize, Skweeze Me Pleeze Me, and arguably Merry Xmas Everybody, are further reasons why young Matthew is now regularly tripped up between lessons and shunned by his classmates and teachers alike.

Indeed, much of the blame for today's teenage texting dyslexia (and perhaps the Rubettes) must surely lie at your stack-heeled feet and I sincerely hope that in order to protect and uphold correct spelling of the English language, your future revival remains far, far away.

Yoorz sarkastiklee

Drk Filpott (Derek Philpott)

....

"Boll okks, wot pray eez rung wiv mee spelling?"

Noddy Holder

Dear Mr. Jagger,
One would recommend at least two strong
undercoats before commencing your intended
DIY task. Failure to do so may lead to the
intended black door actually turning out
purple, owing to the strong primary colour
that you are looking to supersede.

· · ·

The Bee Gees reveal that you are remaining
alive whether you are a brother or whether
you are a mother, thus worryingly foreseeing
curtailed life expectancy for fathers, sons,
uncles, aunts, grandparents, cousins, sisters,
nieces and nephews worldwide.

Dear Was Not Was,

Re: Walk The Dinosaur

Just last week I had to carry our budgerigar's cage from the radiogram in the lounge to our kitchen worktop, so as to gain access to our net curtains and bring them down for cleaning, as they were a bit grubby. As every schoolboy knows, prehistoric animals were the evolutionary prototype for the bird, so perhaps I was not too far off 'walking the dinosaur' (derived from the Greek 'deinos', meaning terrible, and 'sauros', lizard). However, you have expressed a literal desire to attempt to undertake what is in my opinion a ludicrous task, presumably with the animal on some kind of industrial strength leash. Fortunately, Don and Dave, your scheme is rendered impossible by its ill-researched chronological aspect.

I am rather surprised to be entertaining such a scenario, but let us assume that we and said creatures are both occupying either the Triassic period to the end of the Cretaceous, or the Quaternary one, and are living together at the same time, not separated by 65 million years. If you take it upon yourselves to want to travel on foot, each with one such gargantuan reptile totally within your control, either for recreational purposes or, more worryingly, to try to demonstrate that you are 'hard', you are going to face challenges. Achillobators, Velociraptors, Tyrannosaurus Rex and other sauri such as allo- and carcharodonto- are all likely to either wrench your arms off, dine on your still-living frames, or both, before you can begin your expeditions. Should you be (slightly more wisely) considering strolling with a more docile herbivore breed, it is difficult to imagine that a diplodocus or brachiosaurus could be kept still for long enough to slip a vast collar around its neck. If you did manage it, I believe that not only would your 'charge' be oblivious or ignorant to any efforts on your part to steer or manoeuvre it, through verbal commands, jerks or other pressure upon its lead, but that it would be directing *your* course and not vice versa. It must also be borne in mind that these vegetarian sauropods are under constant threat of ambush from their aforementioned meat-eating cousins, and are prone to stampede when being hunted. 'Your' ones will surely not give a fig leaf about you as they frenziedly stomp away from their hungry attackers, in the process tossing you around like rag dolls, dashing and dragging you to your certain demises.

In short, please reconsider your position. If, however, you are hell-bent on sub/dom pedestrian activity with extinct life forms, I suggest that in future you restrict yourselves to affiliations with obsolete species more within your handling capabilities and closer to your size, so as to avoid the pitfalls previously outlined. In line with this less ridiculous plan, future excursions into 'funk lite' may be entitled Perambulate The Quagga, Dawdle The Dodo, Saunter The Great Auk, or Ramble The Crescent Nail-Tailed Wallaby.

Yours,

Derek Philpott (with help from neighbour Wilf Turnbull)

Honorable Gentlemen,

Well, you supposedly jolly gents turn out to be a couple of real sauro-pusses, don'tcha? Walk The Dinosaur was never meant to encourage an unfair or precipitous relationship between pet and owner, quite to the contrary!

In your far too literal reading of the sacred text, you have omitted one ineluctable element: the psychological dominance that Real Men like myself have achieved with all manner of lower life forms – from paramecia to parakeets, rhesus monkeys to Republicans: The Power of the Mind.

As I learned at an early age while watching a first-run screening of the 1973 pimping epic, The Mack – 'Anybody can control a bitch's body: you have to control their minds.' That bauble has seen me through some potentially dangerous situations while strolling with Rex and Diplo, whether the beast in question was male or female – though I must confess the LGBT dinos are tougher to rein in. Inscrutable, I would call them – no insult or injury intended (I don't want to get angry letters!).

And if you must know, I wrote said classic as a love song to my dear firstborn son, Nicholas, who at age five was a bit flummoxed by the notions of eternity and extinction, and wondered aloud thusly: 'Daddy, when the dinosaurs come back again, will we still be here on this earth?' I hemmed and hawed impressively, then assured him the prospect was indeed rather likely, thinking that Old Fred Nietzsche would approve – you know, that whole 'eternal return' business. Quite plausible to a Pythagorean, and to Arthur Eddington acolytes to boot (of whom I know exactly zero, by the way).

Lastly, I don't know what kind of Ed Snowden cyber-rabble you have been consorting with, but obviously some very talented hacker infiltrated the NSA-proof Was (Not Was) Digital Archives located in an underground vault in the Wasatch Mountains of Utah, and confiscated the four song titles you so brazenly revealed to the world in your dismissive missive (so to say).

As long as you promise not to further unveil any priceless couplets from said songs (e.g. Dawdle the Dodo / From Notting Hill to Soho), I will spare you the true prehistoric terror of a call from my very old school attorney, Mr Sol Faigenmoish, Esq. Now that's a guy you don't want to take a walk with once the sun takes its nightly dip in the western waters. You've been warned!

With more fondness than respect, less rancor than stupefaction, I remain yours truly –

David Was

Dear Mr. Amitri,

It is refreshing in this day and age of Lady Gagas, Princes and Marquis Smiths, to encounter a pop star whose very title shuns bogus social elevation and encourages warm familiarity with his 'fanbase'. I too am sometimes referred to by the abbreviatory term for Derek, but normally this informality is reserved for immediate friends and family.

Sadly, I must take issue with one of your 'folksy anthems'. For example, the very fact that Post Office clerks display signs reading 'position closed' and secretaries unplug typewriters and put their coats on are clear indicators, contrary to the title of the piece, that 'nothing ever happens'. The very acts of displaying cashier non-activity notifications and de-activating electrical machinery both entail kinetic energy and the movement of inanimate objects. Furthermore, even were it to be correct that the stylus returns to the song's introduction, said occurrence can only be construed as repetition and not, as you state, a vacuum.

I sincerely hope that you have 'something' to say about these erroneous lyrics in the near future.

Yours,

Derek Philpott

....

Dear Derek,

Many thanks for your enlightening comments on my masterpiece of
gobbledygook, Nothing Ever Happens.

Your points are valid and the general theme of your argument – that
by virtue of describing things happening in the song, the chorus
'Nothing Ever Happens' becomes contradictory – holds much water.

However the 'nothing' to which I allude in the song is really a meta-
phorical 'nothing'. I do not literally mean 'nothing' happens. I mean
to imply, through poetic nuance, that the things I describe 'happening' in the song are really nothing much more than the futile,
meaningless and desperate gestures of a civilisation sleepwalking to
its perdition. For 'nothing', read 'shit-all of any consequence'. Shit-
all of any consequence, however, just wouldn't fit into the rhythm of
the tune, though believe me, I tried very, very hard.

I appreciate your raising of these issues with me and look forward
to resolving any further queries about my lyrics that you may have.

Yours,

JR Currie

Dear The Moody Blues,
In order to create more space in your houses, rather than write letters that you are never meaning to send, you may be better advised to compose the pointless missives as emails which can then be saved to the 'Drafts Folder'.

Taking our seats at the Toby Carvery today, the waiter helpfully asked if we wanted to see the specials. Jean replied that they must have gone down in the world, but yes she would, as long as they played A Message To You, Rudy. This was followed by an awkward silence during which we left the establishment.

Dear The Sweet,
No, I am sorry, I do not know the way to Blockbuster, especially given that the chain went into administration on 16th January. I do, however, know how to subscribe to Sky Movies. Does this help?

Dear The Stereo MCs,

Together with my neighbour Wilf Turnbull, I am arranging a surprise 70th for our friend Gordon Gillard, and having recently heard of you whilst on hold to my network supplier, wonder if you will be available for the evening do, as we believe that having *two* disc jockeys either side of the dance floor, i.e. *Stereo* MCs, instead of the conventional singular, is a novel and innovative idea, given that if one requires a 'comfort break' or even a vol-au-vent, the other can take over, rendering the 'boogie boogie' and 'shout-outs' uninterrupted.

Under normal circumstances we would have approached 'Nothing Else Platters', just off of Commercial Road. However, although their main and suspectedly sole host Pete 'Goes On' Mallard is admittedly very good, his highly inappropriate 'moves' subjected upon the chief bridesmaid at a recent wedding reception in Westcliff during the fifth consecutive dubiously-sourced request for Horny Horny Horny have understandably tarnished his standing within the local community and arguably cost him many booking engagements. Also, Gordon is a keen enthusiast of country and western music, hence we think that your slogan 'to the left, to the right, step it up, step it up', adapted to apply as line dancing instructions pertaining to Achy Breaky Heart and Rednex would be a particular advantage in securing your services in preference.

Prior to confirmation, the Pokesdown & Southbourne Ex-Servicemen's Club committee are insisting on inspection of PAT Testing certificates and public liability documentation, and I regret to inform you that if 'something ain't right' I will reluctantly have to book the busy-handed competitor in your stead. Written confirmation from your good selves to the effect that all extension leads and speaker cables will be secured to the floor by gaffer tape or other effective battening must also be forthcoming; the Entertainment Secretary has made it abundantly clear that the venue will accept no responsibility for any resultant injury claims submitted by peripheral staff or guests should, to quote directly from your 'chilled rave tune', after a 'stumble you might fall' if said trusses are flubbed.

You will hopefully be pleased to learn that there will be no need to 'reach up to the top' when unloading, on the basis that the function will be at 'Ground Level' and there are no stairs involved.

I am also trying to contact Mr Beck as I understand that he has 'two turntables and a microphone', and sounds ideal as a back-up if your equipment for any reason malfunctions.

Subject to your rates being reasonable Wilf and I would be more than willing to send you a non-refundable deposit once reassured that you are completely au fait with the mechanics of the UK postal system. Our wariness stems from your declaration that 'you can't send a forget-me-not', markedly contrasting with the Royal Mail's terms and conditions, which clearly state that perishable items including flowers are suitable for despatch if suitably sealed to prevent leakage, and able to withstand a journey of up to 48 hours.

We look forward to hearing from you subject to the above criteria being to your satisfaction.

Yours,

Derek Philpott

....

Hey Mr Philpott,

Thanks for your letter and request for our DJ spot.

Your extensive queries and demands left us kinda lost for words rather than 'lost in music', but after reflection we figured you're trying to strike a hard bargain so 'I see through you', man.

I'm definite we can satisfy all of your misgivings, even if they are a bit deep down and dirty – we have the capacity to 'move it' when you're concerning yourself with a nice-up dance, but please, no vol-au-vents.

If it is club policy to separate DJs to the left and right, then you'll have to check health and safety about me frisbeeing records across to my partner, Nick, when he requests them, and keep well out of harm's way or you could be 'Playing With Fire', and we don't want no trouble in said disco.

MC Five Alive will deal with the party moves, but I can't vouch for their decency (though he's a regular up in Cambridge's Warning D'n'B

nights, so he can't be that offensive). Just put us up in a nice B&B and put a bottle of Jagermeister on the rider and we'll all be happy in 'The End'.

We're fine with the line dancing and the country and western, providing you provide a mosh pit, as the combination of that and techno is bound to send us jumping off high places and no doubt wanting to 'do it again'.

As for the gaffing down of cables – no prob – and we usually travel with two security to 'keep up the pressure' to whom we have speaker cabinets velcroed to their chests – safe as houses – and troublemakers get a good shake up when approached. To put it short, we guarantee our gear will stay put but I can't take liability for your building, as this heady cocktail of music might play havoc with your foundations after we've been at it 'All Night Long'.

If you really feel the need to take desperate measures in the event of some mash up, I can always do a spot of juggling and Nick knows some Tommy Cooper jokes that I got off the internet, but if you get Mr Beck as back-up, although he's a quality act, he might cost a few bob and does he know any jokes about your mother-in-law? I reckon you'll end up the 'Loser'.

Having heard that your nights are fairly prestigious, boasting a substantial hall of fame on its books, payment should take the form of a second-hand Ford Escort left round the back to avoid any unnecessary paperwork, so I can 'check the new ride out' at the end of what will be a total stimulation of pure 'Creation' of a night.

Can we pencil this one in, Derek?

Best,

Rob

Dear Mr. Kershaw,

'Wouldn't it be good to be in your shoes', you suggest in your catchy offering.

However, I suspect that such a 'footwear exchange' would be less than successful, in that we probably take different sizes. I fear that my size 8 (European size 42) Hush Puppies may chafe your feet after a short while on stage or at home, causing discomfort and blisters. Therefore, I feel that we should both remain in our own choice of footwear for the foreseeable future.

Yours sincerely,

Wilf Turnbull

....

Dear Mr Turnbull,

Thank you for your letter of the 3rd of October.

Whilst I am grateful for your concern regarding my podiatric well-being, I feel it necessary to avail you of the following fact:

It may interest you to learn that I take a size 7 (European size 40) shoe and, therefore, chafing would not be an issue.

Indeed, during the winter months, I find the space available in my shoes insufficient whilst wearing both woollen tights and a thick sock. On these occasions, I respectfully suggest, it *would* be good to be in your shoes (even if it was for just one day).

Yours,

Nik Kershaw

I am rather befuddled by the message they got from the Action Man, to the effect that it's happy and hopes that they are happy, too. I strongly recommend that your friends take him back to the shop, Mr Bowie. When you pull the cord like my son used to, it is supposed to say 'Man patrol, fall in!', 'Enemy Aircraft! Action Stations!', 'Enemy in sight, range 1,000' and 'Commander to base, request support!'

'I will follow you, will you follow me?', enquire Genesis. I must make a mental note never to drive to an unknown destination with Collins and his cohorts, which would probably result in us either driving around in a big circle or being stuck on a roundabout.

Dear All About Eve,

Re: Martha's Harbour

I recently 'picked up' your 'eponymous long player' quite by mistake at a car boot sale, thinking, quite understandably seeing that I had come out with the wrong spectacles, that it was the much sought after replacement disc that I had been searching for since our 'The Marilyn Collection' box set was inexcusably returned to us incomplete by some now former Gala Bingo partners, Alicia and Nigel Saxtonhouse. On the plus side, however, my wife Jean and I were delighted to find a job lot of 'nearly new' curtain fabric in the back of a Peugeot Partner which will be perfect for our conservatory. In addition, we are both now pleasantly surprised to be very fond of your maudlin ode to a biblical figure referencing boat storage cove, and its 'stripped back arrangement', although unfortunately after several exposures I now feel compelled to write to you outlining my concerns pertaining to its 'lyrical content'.

Thanks to a particularly fallacious dithyramb as vocalised by your 'lead singer', I have had to spend some considerable time this morning (which was scheduled to be enjoyed relaxing with two soft-boiled eggs, a slice of Kingsmill and a repeat of Booze Patrol Australia on Watch TV) reassuring Jean that my occasional golfing weekends with my next door but one neighbour Gordon Gillard are just that. It is, thank heavens, patently clear to her on the other hand that I am anything *but* an organic coalescence contoured by the manifest abrasion of mistrals across an expanse of saline fluid comprising a vast majority of our planet's hydrosphere. Sadly, it took until the Antipodean random breath test programme's end credits before my wife could be convinced that in addition to not being an ocean wave (I am, in actual fact, a retired printer) I was, in addition, not your love.

It is also worthy of note that the enforcement of unpaid labour on sea vessels, much favoured by King Louis XIV as a means of expanding his fleet, was last documented as being practised by the Barbary corsairs in the late 19th century, therefore in order for you to be a galley slave, as you attest, I am estimating that you would have had to have attained, at the very youngest, an age of 89 years at the time of your initially static appearance on television in 1988. If this is the case, then the BBC make up department are to be commended for the achievement of such a youthful presentation, and your inability to hear the music owing to your advancement in years is entirely understandable.

With regard to the last observation, you may be interested to learn that we recently invited our friends Wilf and Olive Turnbull to Philpott Place for a 'Top Of The Pops Evening', in which we re-enacted many memorable moments from the show's history.

These included Wilf writing the words to Shaddap Your Face in marker pen onto the reverse side of some old wallpaper blu-tacked to his new Toshiba 46 inch TV screen and encouraging us to sing along while he pointed to them with an extended steel tape measure, and the four of us tearing up pre-printed A4 photocopies of John Travolta before launching into Rat Trap, replete with Olive blowing into a slightly opened folding brolly to compensate for our failure to procure a candelabra saxophone. We then went out to the back garden for three minutes to replicate the refusal of The Clash to take part, but by far the most authentic homage of the evening was to your good selves, whereby Jean and I sat on the high breakfast bar stools in our kitchen, draped in the material we purchased at the same time as your CD, looking at each other quizzically for a full 86 seconds after Wilf had put it on in the front room.

Notwithstanding this awkward broadcast, which we all concede to be no fault of your own, Jean, Wilf, Olive and I wish you all the best in your future endeavours but would recommend that all upcoming concerts be of a pre-recorded nature!

Yours sincerely,

Derek Philpott

....

From the desk of:
Ms Julianne Regan,
Narnia,
Behind-The-Wardrobe.

Wednesday, 25 September 2013

Dear Mr Philpott,

Namaste!

You cannot imagine the delight and relief I felt at receiving your missive. Do bear with me while I contextualise this for you!

Less than one month ago, my country seat was burgled. I was up in London on important business, id est, discussing the possibility of an appearance on the once popular television show, Never Mind The

Buzzcocks. As tempting as the offer was of an overnight stay at the Hammersmith Novotel on the date of recording and as many salted snacks as I could consume and as much Prosecco as I could imbibe in the 'green room', pre and post show, I turned down the mooted public ridicule. As you will know from the Top of the Pops incident you mention in your letter, or Marthagate, as I am wont to call it, I am no stranger to public humiliation. However, I feel a line should be drawn between being victim to an innocent audio mishap (for which some hapless sound technician was probably fired) and willingly placing myself under the scrutiny of a 'panel' of C-list celebrities who frankly would not know a song if it subjected them to an enthusiastic frottage on the Bakerloo Line, in tourist season! (Had the marvellously witty Simon Amstell still been hosting the show, I may have been cajoled.)

I digress. On returning home I found the lower ground sash window had been forced and had been the point of entry for the thieves. My collection of Wade Whimsies were strewn across my novelty Sergeant Pepper rug, and one of my favourites, the 'land cockerel', had been stamped upon and lay atop the moustache of George, undoubtedly the most spiritual Beatle, this 'tableau' seeming all the more poignant for that.

I shall spare you further detail and cut to the chase. My vinyl record collection had vanished. The thieves had made off with the lot, some items of which I know I shall never be able to replace. Now, some might perceive me as someone who spends much time away with the proverbial fairies, my thoughts all lofty and poetic and not of this earth, yet they'd be wrong, Mr Philpott, very wrong. I am, in modern vernacular, pretty 'streetwise' and had daubed SmartWater on the sleeves of all said vinyl records. I'm not sure how this works, I shall ask my insurers, but there will be some way you can detect this on the sleeves. Might I ask if you would do this for me? Naturally I am not accusing you of the theft – perish that thought! But I believe that thieves do use car boot sales as a means of offloading their swag onto unsuspecting and decent people like your good self and dear lady wife. Should the items be traceable back to me, I would happily reimburse you for your troubles and for the cost of postage and packing. If you would be kind enough to at least return my All About Eve albums, my signed copy of Quiet Life by the fragrant and ahead-of-their-time band Japan, and my AC/DC boxed set, the rest, I think, I can replace.

And now to the lyrical content of the song Martha's Harbour. It is regrettable that your wife, Jean, felt she had cause for suspicion as to your fidelity. It's not in my nature to pry, but simply out of concern for your future relationship together I feel I should ask if Jean has previously wondered about whether you might 'dally'? I'm not one of these pierced heavy-booted hardcore feminist types, I assure you (although I am grateful for the vote), but men and women can often seem like they are at opposite ends of an emotional spectrum. On this subject you may wish to visit some of my latter works: a song called Infra Red, which could be seen as male at one end of the electromagnetic spectrum, and Ultraviolet, the album title, being at the other, female. I hope you and Jean can inhabit a mutually happy hypothetical place somewhere in the middle on this spectrum, a place of trust. Failing that, a bouquet of garage flowers and a box of Elizabeth Shaw Mint Crisp will often heal a marital rift.

On your well-made and historically accurate point regarding the cessation of the need for 'galley slaves' – I admit that the mention of said slave in the context of the song was not purely placed there as a vehicle to carry a theme of yearning, of servitude, of inconsequentiality against colossal might, but also because 'slave' rhymes with 'wave'. I did not wish to confuse the listener by bringing a 'Dave' into the narrative. The imaginary lover in the tale might have been called Dave, but that would serve to personalise the song far too sharply and, if you'll excuse me for cheapening my art by referencing money, makes the song less coverable. (I still hope for a call from Celine Dion's 'people' on that count.) It also limits the possibility of the song being synchronised for use in TV adverts, perchance for Findus, Birds Eye, DFDS Seaways or P&O Ferries (if they still are in operation?). Other than 'Dave', words I considered were brave, cave, crave, flavour, gave, grave etc. and mentally travelled the entire alphabet, right up to the word 'Zave', a Zimbabwean town with a population of less than 1000. Zimbabwe being landlocked would have made pursuance of this idea difficult, to say the least. So in my defence, let me say that I didn't settle on the use of 'galley slave' lightly.

I hope this letter goes some way to assure you that I am aware of the shortcomings of the song lyric. How fortuitous it might have been had I known someone like you back in the late 80s, with such sharpness of mind and who might have just placed a friendly hand on my shoulder and quietly said, 'You know, love, you might want to look that over once more before you commit it to 2 inch master tape.' We might now be discussing a number one hit rather than a number ten. Hindsight is a wonderful thing.

Yours, humbled,

Julianne

PS I have just learnt from my lovely caseworker at Victim Support that I should consider myself lucky that it was only a crushed Wade cockerel that I found upon George's moustache, as it seems nervous thieves often defecate at the scene of their crime. To have returned home to a turd atop the 'tache would have been utterly horrendous. I don't hold out much hope for the perpetrators of the crime to be brought to justice. Victim Support tells me that many 'youths' steal in order to raise monies to spend on drugs. Had I known that, I could have just left a note on the telephone table saying: 'Three months' supply of antidepressant medication can be found on the top shelf of the cabinet in the bathroom. Enjoy!' and still be in possession of my vinyl. Hey ho, we live and learn!

Not the Perfect Slugs! They're **Nine Inch Snails!**

Feed him on Simply Bread! **Mick Ducknall**

'I sat on the roof and looked at the mouse.' **Owlton John**

Hatched this way!
Lady Budgerie-Gaga

Do you really want to
hook me? **Koi George**

Put your little paw in mine. **Bunny And Hare**

This is Hardboiled! **Jarvis Cockerel**

Never Mind the Bulldogs, here's **Johnny Rottweiler!**

There ain't no gibbons in this band! **Chimpan-ZZ Top**

Fur it up! **Bobcat Marley**

Parallel Equines! **Zebra Harry**

No, no, no, no. Don't Flock
With My Heart. **Wool-i-Lamb**

It's not Bungle in the Jungle.
It's **Ian Pandason!**

With no particular place to growl.
Chuck Beary

Hay Ho! Let's Go!
Gee Gee Ramone

We are the rodent crew.
Lemming

Not 'In The Cage'. **Cheetah Gabriel**

Dear Peter Perrett,

Re: Another Girl, Another Planet

I was quite alarmed to hear on Jools Holland today that space travels in your blood, but am pleased to advise you, antithetical to your fallacious despondency, that there *is* something that you can do about it.

It is clear from my extensive research on your behalf this afternoon into many learned authorities but mainly the NHS Choices website, that the transiting arterial void to which you refer is most likely the interior of an air bubble or embolism, which malady, whose symptoms include acute disorientation and extreme fatigue, may well induce the sensation of being located upon a commensurate orbiting body accompanied by an unfamiliar female, looking ill, and long journeys wearing you out.

Rather than 'flirt with death', it is therefore strongly recommended that you call an ambulance immediately, sir, with a view to being taken straight to the nearest hospital. Under no circumstances should an unreliable vehicle be used to speed you to an out of the way infirmary, thereby risking your 'Breaking Down', 'Miles From Nowhere'.

Yours,

Derek Philpott

....

Dear Mr Philpott,

Having seen your long list of contributors, I am most disappointed (nay, almost insulted) that it has taken you so long to contact me with your serene and much-appreciated advice.

I have vast experience in these matters... I once delivered a dead 'Richard Lloyd', at the speed of sound, to Lewisham Hospital. They

did a remarkable job in reviving him as, I am told, he is still living an almost-human life to this day.

Thank you for your communication; it has been read and processed.

Love,

Peter Perrett

PS Be Safe

DEAR COLONEL ABRAMS,
ALTHOUGH I WAS SORRY TO HEAR OF YOUR
CURRENT PREDICAMENT, I MUST TAKE ISSUE
WITH THE FACT THAT YOU EQUATE BEING
TRAPPED TO BEING LIKE A FOOL IN A
CAGE. I CAN ASSURE YOU THAT MANY
HIGHLY INTELLIGENT PEOPLE HAVE BEEN
INCARCERATED, ALTHOUGH ADMITTEDLY THE
ONLY ONE THAT SPRINGS TO MIND AT THE
MOMENT IS HANNIBAL LECTER, WHO IS A
FICTIONAL CHARACTER. NEVERTHELESS, THE
INFERENCE THAT ONLY THOSE OF A LOW IQ
MAY BE PLACED INTO CUSTODY IS ONE THAT
REQUIRES CORRECTION.

DEAR BEYONCE,
AS IT IS A NICE DAY I AM ON MY WAY TO
WILTSHIRE, AND CURRENTLY ON MY PASSENGER
SEAT IS MY PACKED LUNCH. I MUST ASSURE
YOU THAT A PACKET OF TAYTOS, A CHEESE
AND PICKLE SANDWICH, A CHICKEN LEG AND A
TOPIC ARE NOT EVERYTHING I OWN, ALTHOUGH
I MUST GRANT YOU THAT THE BOX IS TO THE
LEFT, TO THE LEFT.

Dear Frank Turner,

Re: The Road

As much as my wife Jean and I admire your 'troubadour anthem', Mr Turner, it is with regret that I must inform you that it includes some 'Tell Tale Signs' that your expedition could conclude with disastrous results.

Firstly, to reveal that one keeps a small bag full of clothes carefully stored, somewhere secret, somewhere safe, somewhere close to the door, could be interpreted as a catalyst for 'The Real Damage' on several levels. Disclosure of the diminutive garment holdall's very existence to your live 'following' and the whole world at large via Eyetunes 'downloads', let alone a near thorough revelation of its co-ordinates, now renders the relief of all vestment carrier clandestinity highly probable. Indeed, with the benefit of hindsight it is arguable that any future habiliment haversack or some such declassification could be avoided if you were to 'Hold Your Tongue', a laudable characteristic which you 'Must Try Harder', Mr. Turner, to acuminate.

It ought to be appended that, far from being devoid of peril, the situation of such a concealed compact attire impediment so proximate to an entranceway is not careful at at all. It is, surely, for anyone who tries to place 'One Foot Before The Other' without looking where they are going, and, if you will pardon the journey-related pun, a 'trip hazard'.

Finally, it is to be conceded, by the very fact of the illusive plateaux fully encircling one's location at all times, that said land/sky convergence is, as you correctly imply, omnipresent. That said, Mr Turner, and contrary to your throaty assertions, I am afraid that your claims to both face the horizon everywhere you go, and live on it, must be contested for the following reasons:

a) Your earth/atmosphere dovetailing lineality not being open to question ought to be countered by its regularly being obscured by limits in human vision, as well as indoor 'gig' venues and similar walls, fences, other buildings, and computer or mobile telephone fascia when texting or 'tweeting' to your 'fan base'.

b) By the very nature that an unattainable vista must be situated at a considerable distance from the observer to be viewed, it therefore stands to reason that under no circumstances could it ever be reached, let alone inhabited or, for that matter, fitted with a door (see paragraphs 2 and 3 above).

I sincerely hope that you do not mind my bringing this critique to your attention, Mr Turner, but being somewhat experienced in these matters I feel duty-bound to 'Pass It Along'. It is, to use 'Four Simple Words', for better or worse, and 'The Way I Tend To Be'.

I remain yours sincerely,

Derek Philpott

....

Dear Derek,

Thanks very much for your thoughtful letter. You raise some substantive points about my song, The Road, and I'd like to address them individually, and in full.

Firstly, you note that I've slightly given away the location of my secret bag of clothes. However, I have more cunning than you give me credit for; I am, in fact, a decorated, medal-winning Hiding Enthusiast.

My ability to hide things from prying eyes is legendary and recognised by several European and international sporting establishments. I won a bronze medal for hiding Scotch eggs at the 1998 Nagano Winter Olympics. My strategies for hiding things include, among many others, misdirection. Thus it is that there is a dummy bag of clothes – in fact my laundry basket – close to my door, positioned in such a way as to appear to have been hidden by an amateur. The

potential saboteur would thus find him or herself not only failing to take my actual bag of tour clothes, but also in possession of my dirty underwear. Advantage Turner!

I also could, if you think about it, be bluffing about the whole 'near the door' thing anyway.

Moving on to the second, rather more metaphysical issue – the location and habitability of the horizon. While I take your point that, arguably, one is both constantly facing the horizon, and unlikely to see much of it in a built urban environment, I fear you may have missed the thrust of my argument. If one was to lie down, either facing straight up to the ceiling or sky, or face down towards the ground, one would not be facing the horizon. I suffer from a rare congenital defect that means that I have to, at all times, refrain from facing directly up or down – otherwise I am prone to severe lapses of sartorial taste and/or dizzying bouts of verbal diarrhoea. We all have our crosses to bear.

Thankfully, the end result of this affliction is that I am usually facing the direction that I'm travelling, and thus rarely trip over.

The second part of your criticism – that one could not, arguably, inhabit the horizon, or indeed affix it with a door, is a fair cop. I'll do my best to make more sense in future.

Thanks for your letter, all the best to Jean.

Yours,

Frank

Dear Midnight Oil,
In response to your rather dim-witted enquiry, I
must say 'You don't!! Now get up immediately and call
the fire brigade!!'

Dear Mr. Robinson,

Re: 2-4-6-8 Motorway

Although algebra was not one of my strong points at school, I have to say that even *I* could have got this one, Tom; Motorway clearly represents the number 10 as the next in the sequence. I look forward to your next teaser, and feel free to make it a little harder next time.

Yours,

Derek Philpott (and Wilf Turnbull)

....

Dear Mr Philpott (and Mr Turnbull),

Thank you for your kind enquiry dated September 23 about my little mathematical conundrum.

The solution to my Punk Period Puzzle is, as you correctly state, simple enough – but alas, your answer falls some way short of the mark. It's not so much your former weakness in algebra as a schoolboy that has betrayed you, but a regrettable failure to grasp the principle of negative numbers.

In fact, the sum is set out quite straightforwardly in the song title, i.e. two minus four minus six minus eight. The answer, plain to anyone of even remotely mathematical bent, is that Motorway equals minus sixteen.

However, if you'd like a slightly more taxing teaser to while away the long winter evenings, perhaps you could apply yourself to the mathematical solution for 'double white line' in the third line of the chorus. Even I haven't been able to work out the answer to that one.

Please pass on my best wishes to Olive and Jean.

Your sincerely,

Tom Robinson

Newport Pagnall Maths Institute
Buckinghamshire
MK16 0QP

Dear Right Said Fred,

We decided to have fajitas for a change last night, Right Said Fred, and all was going well until Jean ('She's My Missus') embarked on her second trip to the lounge, having already fetched the chicken and tortillas in. My wife is very agile on her feet and I often marvel at her adroit manoeuvrability, but sadly, despite the curves she got, Jean then dropped the side dishes and drinks on the way from the kitchen after crossing the path of our ten-year-old tortoiseshell Gladys, some might say 'on the catwalk, yeah, on the catwalk'.

Although the chilli rice and jalapeños were just about salvageable, my clockwise aforementioned chums, the circular serving tray was unfortunately shattered and, acutely mindful of the fillets going cold in the other room, we were forced 'Without Thinking' to make do with scraping what was left in the fridge into 'Those Simple Things', a couple of eggcups. It was, however, my easterly facing pals, soon made all too 'Obvious' that 'It's Not The Way' to present up sour cream, salsa and guacamole. Although the sharp point of each could be lowered in with ease, when either of us would 'Stick It Out', it was to find our

Dorito dry, on account of its equilateral contours restricting all contact with the now elusive base of said breakfast receptacle.

It was therefore not without poignancy that your 'UK Smash' Deeply Dippy, referencing as it did the very essence of our dining predicament, should then come on the radio in an advert for a local paddling pool company, prompting us to investigate your work further, Right Said Fred.

Although your declaration that you are 'too sexy' for your love is not open to debate (especially after our just having watched Holiday Love Rats Exposed on Channel 5 featuring various, shall we say, aesthetically mismatched youths and divorced retirees), one must take issue with several of your other over-abundant allurement assertions.

For example, I am bamboozled as to precisely how you are able to be too sexy for your shirt and hat, and *will* tell you what I think about that. Neither buttonable upper body garmentry nor headgear are notorious for their competitive lustful provocativeness. With regard to the former, however, it is fully concedable that 'it hurts' either if it is several sizes too small or is new and still has the pins in.

Also, unless there has been any recent tightening on immigration controls of which we were not aware, excessive sensuality or 'hotness' is unlikely at passport control to deny one access to Milan, New York and Japan*.

Furthermore, my dextral friends, my 70th was attended by, amongst others, my next door but one neighbour Gordon's grandson, who is currently under contract to the Damart catalogue people given that he is a model ('you know what I mean') and, as well as sharing your reticence to 'disco dance' on the night, has a great number of female admirers. I must therefore challenge your claim to be inordinately tantalising for my, or indeed any party, bar perhaps, based upon their current Prospective Parliamentary Candidates, the SDP.

On grounds of common decency I am relieved to learn that you are unduly sultry for your cat.

On an extraneous note regarding Don't Talk Just Kiss, one sincerely hopes that you are not considering a change in career, Right Said Fred. The substitution of speech with such an over-familiar act could well prove troublesome in job interviews, especially for the posts of lecturer and schoolteacher.

I have to say 'Night Night' now, chaps. For some inexplicable reason, since looking at your pop videos Jean has decided that she *does* want a couple of boiled eggs.

Yours,

Derek Philpott

* If you are in fact referencing the pop group Japan, my pop star friend Julianne Regan wishes to convey the following to you: 'Yeh, in your dreams!'

....

Dear Mr Philpott,

It is with great merriment and delight that I am in receipt of your correspondence. That said, upon reading it I must add concern and consternation to my emotional menu.

I propose to respond to you in chronological order.

I fear any other approach with regards to my response could add confusion to an already disorderly world.

Mexican food should always be approached with caution. Two aspects of your culinary-themed evening are immediately apparent.

Firstly, you have conveniently omitted Jean's frequent imbibing of Mexico's favourite beer, Negra Modelo, during her many unsupervised trips to the kitchen. Secondly, you failed to carry out a full reconnaissance of the terrain including the probability of a lounging moggie.

With Jean's penchant for Mexico's finest I would have thought a clear and unencumbered entry and exit route should have been at the top of your to-do list.

These two omissions in my opinion add an unfavourable parallax to the evening.

Deeply Dippy is indeed a poignant reference for your dining extravaganza, thank you for that observation! Dips are a large part of the South of the Border experience as well as your wife Jean who, in all honesty, seems to embody the phrase, albeit unwittingly.

Poor Jean.

Onto I'm Too Sexy....

Of course on the face of it, and to the untrained ear, I'm Too Sexy is a repetitive, quirky ditty poking fun at those much-maligned cadavers, professional models.

Or so you'd like you to think........

In reality, I'm Too Sexy is a labyrinth of wordplay and an encrypted narrative.

The opening line 'I'm too sexy for my love' is of course a desperate plea from the wandering lost soul of Narcissus himself. Too much beauty for one man to bear..!!

'I'm too sexy for my shirt' and later in the song 'I'm too sexy for my hat' is a clear rejection of the material chains we have allowed clothes to become. Slaves, if you will, to the giant looms and the corporations that produce them. And yes, 'it hurts', it bloody well hurts…!!!!!

'I'm too sexy for New York, Milan and Japan' is an experimental leap into the world of finance. At this point I must add we knew we were throwing the listener an unexpected curve. It answers the many unanswered questions of the 1987 financial crash as well as serving a prophetic role in the warning of the 2008 financial crisis........you're welcome!

In this crazy, mixed up planet we all find ourselves on, we felt some plain talking and free thinking could do the world of good.

So with this thought in mind the refrain 'I'm a model, you know what I mean' is a 'real life' quote from a female model we were friends with. At this point in the song it was time to give the listener the licence to throw caution to the wind. I hasten to add, a different kind of wind from the one you and Jean may have encountered after your Mexican dinner!!

Our reticence to 'disco dance' is also from real life. Sadly I can't go into specifics as the court case is still pending.

Cats are and have always been the most enigmatic of creatures. We thought it only fitting to reference them with the respect and reverence they clearly deserve.

I agree Don't Talk Just Kiss is a mantra we could all benefit from, from time to time.

As you wisely point out, a meeting with the bank manager or contesting a parking ticket with a traffic warden would not be an appropriate setting.

We hope we've managed to shed some light into the complex world of pop songs and the wacky carefree folk that deliver them to your radios and other listening devices.

Many thanks for your letter.

Health, love and happiness from the house of Right Said Fred.

Fred and Richard xx

Dear Ms. Wilde,

Re: Kids in America

With regard to the ponderings contained within your jaunty offering, which Jean and I enjoy considerably, I am pleased to be able to shed light on some, but not all, of said conundrums presented.

You refer to wondering why you are seated unaccompanied whilst surveying fast moving traffic through the vantage point of a tarnished dormer.

It is, if you will pardon the pun, 'clearly' apparent that the dirty old window that you allude to has not been washed for some time, perhaps due to neglect on the part of yourself, the landlord/owner of the property and/or a slovenly outside contractor, and the cars in the city go rushing by owing to you possibly viewing a main road leading to a metropolis used by heavy traffic exceeding the speed limit in a bid to hurriedly reach the drivers' respective destinations. Also, the volume of vehicular activity will obviously be far greater if you observe an arterial thoroughfare and the rapid movement of automobiles at a time synonymous with peak hour commuting, i.e. a Friday night when everyone's moving, or between the hours of 8–9.30 on a weekday morning. It is to be posited that you are bereft of companionship as a result of some of the other Kids in America perhaps popping out to eat a cheeseburger and 'fries' or embarking on a trip to Walmart for 'groceries'.

I hope that the above will be of assistance and satisfy your musings.

Whilst writing, please allow me to state that I am most impressed by your powers of meteorological precognition. Whether they be born of clairvoyance and/or an advanced knowledge of anomalous Atlantic tidal patterns, vis-à-vis an impending hitherto unreferenced tsunami affecting the most densely populated city in the 'Land of the Free' through to the most inland point of The Beach Boys' home state, Jean and I are anxious to learn of the new wave from New York to

East California's approximate date. This is in order that our impending 'vacation' to The Grand Canyon may be timed to avoid the catastrophic deluge which, although marring our panoramic view, may ironically cause any accidental fall into the National Monument to be slightly safer for any hapless tourists. Please do not 'keep us hanging on' in the impartation of this information, as we intend to book our flights imminently.

Best regards,

Derek Philpott

....

Dear Derek,

Thank you sincerely for your letter. I am so glad that yourself and Jean enjoy the song; I like to think we're all kids at heart, and not just 'Kids in America'.

Given your almost encyclopedic knowledge of all things 'pop' I'm sure the fact that I was not responsible for the lyrics in question will not have escaped your attention. Nonetheless, I am grateful to you for taking the time to attempt to shed light on some of the song's intrinsic puzzles.

Regarding the window, it isn't apparent whether or not the window is dirty on the inside, the outside or, indeed, both (the only thing being certain is that my view would have been obscured in some way) yet I can categorically state that it would not have been as a result of any lack of hygiene on my part – that's not how my mum raised me.

Similarly, although I must confess that the mental image of several thousand tourists enjoying a refreshing dip in a water-filled Grand Canyon is quite fascinating, I'm afraid I must shatter your illusion as to your perception of my powers of meteorological precognition.

The 'wave' in question is not – as I'm sure you are aware – actually a tsunami. Whilst a wave can, indeed, refer to 'a ridge or a swell moving through or along the surface of a large body of water…', it can also be 'a sudden occurrence of or increase in a phenomenon, feeling, or emotion…' and I rather suspect that this second definition of the noun is the appropriate one to apply in this case and it is far from being a warning of impending danger.

You do, however, raise one very valid point; others, too, have wondered why the said wave was predicted to arrest itself some distance short of the Californian coastline, rendering the inhabitants of the western side of the Beach Boys' home state (as you poetically describe it) bereft. Unfortunately this particular conundrum remains a mystery to everyone, including me ;)

With very best wishes,

Kim Wilde

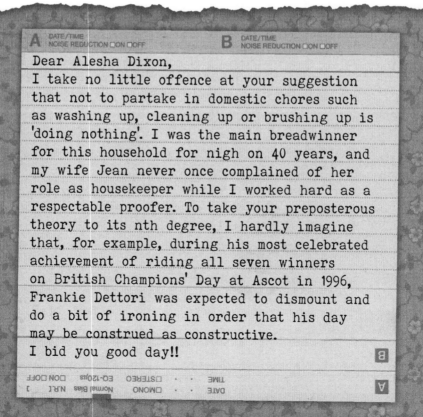

A DATE/TIME NOISE REDUCTION ☐ON ☐OFF   B DATE/TIME NOISE REDUCTION ☐ON ☐OFF

Dear Alesha Dixon,
I take no little offence at your suggestion that not to partake in domestic chores such as washing up, cleaning up or brushing up is 'doing nothing'. I was the main breadwinner for this household for nigh on 40 years, and my wife Jean never once complained of her role as housekeeper while I worked hard as a respectable proofer. To take your preposterous theory to its nth degree, I hardly imagine that, for example, during his most celebrated achievement of riding all seven winners on British Champions' Day at Ascot in 1996, Frankie Dettori was expected to dismount and do a bit of ironing in order that his day may be construed as constructive.
I bid you good day!!

Dear Space,

Re: Neighbourhood

I am afraid, my continuous area-homaging amigos, that I have several pressing concerns pertaining to the community in which you reside which I feel duty-bound to impart.

Firstly, if you are adamant that in 666 there lives a Mister Miller who is your local vicar and a serial killer, the non-disclosure of this information to the police force may well implicate you as accessories to any further cleric-initiated atrocities.

As regards your statement relating to the transvestite at number 69 who is a man by day and a woman by night, whilst I do not doubt that the 'cross-dresser' may *clothe* diurnally in masculine attire and nocturnally in feminine garb, the matter of whether a gender reversal operation is performed every early evening, on account of the strains on both the NHS and one's 'downstairs' should be open to question.

Furthermore, your statement that you 'will all be waiting when the bulldozers come', and 'in a neighbourhood like this you know it's hard to survive so you'd (presumably, once again, the bulldozer) better come prepared 'cause they won't take us alive', is, I fear, a perplexing paradox. It may reasonably be countered that by being prepared to unsuccessfully obstruct an oncoming excavator, the endurance to which you refer must surely be jeopardised by your JCB-martyrdom expiry willingness.

In conclusion, I hope you will forgive me stating that, far from being 'a beautiful neighbourhood', the combination of such a multitude of dubious personalities and other undesirables residing in this very long road may render it the most unsavoury thoroughfare since Benefits Street.

Yours,

Derek Philpott

Dear Derek,

OK, I'll give it a go.

Well, about the vicar, I used to be one of his favourite choirboys, if you get my drift, so I could hardly go to the cops, could I?

Regarding the said trannie, he was also the top drug dealer in our street so he could easily afford to go private.

As you might know, Space are dead hard Scousers so a pathetic bull-dozer don't scare us, and our neighbourhood is beautiful coz we FRIGGIN SAY SO!!!

Yours,

Tommy

Dear Saxon,

Re: Wheels of Steel

I very much admire your rock anthem, as I am a keen motorist myself. I currently own a Nissan Micra, which is perhaps rather less powerful than your '68 Chevy', although you omit to provide us with the exact model of your vehicle.

I regret, however, that your enthusiasm for its 'Wheels of Steel' is misplaced, as surely they can be considered standard on a motor car of this vintage. Unless I am mistaken, I think you will find that the alternative of alloy wheels was not developed until after the date of the vehicle's manufacture. (Of course, steel is itself an alloy, although it is not usually referred to as such by wheel enthusiasts.) I presume that you are not equally excited by other unsurprising features, such as the car's 'indicators' or 'windscreen wipers'.

In addition, you appear to advocate reckless or dangerous motoring, despite your tuneful delivery. 'One-forty', whether kilometres or miles per hour, is far beyond the speed limit on any public highway in the United Kingdom; moreover, you boast of forcing another driver off the road, merely because he attempted to obstruct you in some way. One also certainly hopes that there *is* no looking back when your 'foot's on the throttle'. The deployment of acceleration whilst in charge of any motor vehicle, be it even a golf buggy, demands that the driver be forward facing throughout.

I am disappointed with your attitude, Saxon, and would suggest that you read the Highway Code as a matter of urgency.

Despite the above concerns, I remain fond of your work, which often seems to have a 'transport' theme. I certainly look forward to future offerings which may feature coaches, trams or milk floats.

Yours sincerely,

Wilf Turnbull (with help from Derek Philpott)

....

My dear Mr Philpott,

I must say, I was most happy to receive your recent correspondence; my mailbox is all too often filled to the brim with back issues of Pigeon Fanciers' Weekly and Ratting Gazette.

Amid the dexterous wordsmithery of your lengthy missive, I couldn't help but notice the phrase 'Highway Code', and thought I might take the liberty of addressing this first. As far as I am aware, no such publication exists in the sovereign territory of South Yorkshire. I understand legislation is in the pipeline, but any codes made law only currently apply to whippets and ferrets. Being a fair-minded Yorkshireman, not to mention a Nissan enthusiast, I am, however, more than happy to be schooled further in the draconian legislation

that has been implemented beyond our fair Yorkshire borders, tha' knows.

I humbly take your point regarding our blatant usage of the word 'steel' in our composition, and can only hope to temper your ire by explaining that it is also meant to invoke the bygone days of steel manufacture in the nearby metropolitan sprawl of Sheffield (known more popularly to outsiders as 'Sheffield Nil' after the football team). In the interests of even-handedness, I should point out that the city boasts a second football team, known as Sheffield Wednesday, named after the one day working week introduced during the dark days of Thatcherism.

It may also be a good time to note that the phrase 'Wheels of Steel' has been rather ironically usurped to advertise DJ nights of late. I understand it purports to the twin record decks that is their stock in trade. That's as may be, but you can't lean into a curve at 100 miles per hour on a Dansette. If I may speak frankly, Mr Philpott, I really don't know where the music business is heading of late. I fully expect a whammy bar to mean some kind of pick up joint in the very near future, and I'll have to go back to a basic fixed bridge arrangement on my signature guitar to avoid guilt by association.

I would like to take this occasion to point out that Saxon also recorded a song called Iron Wheels, and as such we feel most strongly that the band should be viewed through the prism of equal opportunity metallurgic championing.

Thanking you once again for your timely letter, sir; I find myself in your debt. You may not be aware, but I am a collector of fine bone china of antique vintage, and your expectation of a short ditty extolling the virtues of the humble milk float has got me thinking. I feel a song coming on, perhaps lauding the humble antiques dealer, flying down the highway in an ecologically sound electric buggy, his precious hand-painted cups and saucers gently rattling in safety, cocooned in the plastic milk crates…shouting 'sithee' as he exits the environs of Goldthorpe. Perhaps not.

I remain, Stalwartly Yorkshire, Metal and Proud, and thank you for your pointers, though I suspect they are of very little use for ratting. You need terriers for that.

May your tea be strong and your lavatories external,

Graham Oliver

Dear The Jam,
I was dismayed to learn on the radio today that there is an 'A Bomb' in Wardour Street, especially considering that this is a popular spot for tourists that will need to be evacuated immediately. You are to be commended for bringing the existence of this device to our attention. However, rather than heading to a recording studio to record a 'power pop anthem' about it, forgive me for stating that a 999 call to the emergency services would have been the most sensible option. This is indeed the most foolhardy case of timewasting since Mr. Springsteen similarly informed me that he was ablaze.

Dear Mr John,
In accordance with your instruction, I HAVE told everyone that 'Your Song' is indeed my song. However, I have just been informed by your solicitors to desist in these proclamations on the basis of copyright infringement, and that I will not be entitled to any royalties. But then again, STILL no — I DO mind, I DO mind!

Dear The Piranhas,

Re: Tom Hark

Whilst concurring, as stated in your faux-ska hit Tom Hark, that life is directly the opposite to death, i.e. you have to live or else you'd die, I take issue with your assertion that I have to laugh or else I'd cry. Quantification that jollity and sobbing are the only emotions known to the Homo sapien is direly needed. For example, I am currently writing this on my computer typewriter straight-faced, which could be construed as a limbo state.

I might also point out that your attempts to build your holiday plans around World War Three are most futile, given that in the event of global conflict it is unlikely that most travel agents and airlines would be permitted or indeed motivated to continue trading. Furthermore, from personal experience I can confirm that closing one's eyes and counting to ten is likely to *exacerbate* rather than 'vanish away' trage-dies, as I learned to my cost on a dry ski slope in Middlesex in 1978.

As regards your observation that 'they want you in the army but you just can't go, you're far too busy listening to your radio', not only is this attitude cowardly but I fail to see that a preoccupation with Terry Wogan et al could excuse your enforced conscription.

Now pack your bags!

Yours,

Derek Philpott

....

Hello Mr Philpott,

Your description of Tom Hark is very appropriate. It could indeed be considered 'faux ska' as it is a kwela song from southern Africa,

which I believe to be several inches away from Jamaica on most peoples' maps.

The line 'You have to laugh or else you cry' was aimed at the 360,000 people who purchased the single in the mistaken belief that it was a ska song, only to be disabused of that erroneous notion by the sleeve notes, only to become instantly bipolar.

With regard to my travel plans, I would like to point out that my concerns were identical to your own, in as much as I considered it likely that international travel post-holocaust might be troublesome, and I wished to holiday in advance of that nuisance.

My comment about 'closing one's eyes and counting to ten' was a subtle reference to airlines' recommendation that people should put their heads between their legs just prior to a crash, not to increase their chances of survival, but to increase the chances of identification of the corpses via dental records. (I once played a gig in a dry ski slope 'apres ski' and, with all due respect, I saw no literature encouraging skiers to engage in any counting or eye closing, with the tacit exception of blinking, whilst braving the bristles and the gravity.)

In defence of my cowardice, I need only quote from another lyric I wrote:
Please don't recruit me
Bullets pollute me
And green don't suit me
I look like death

In response to your closing remark, I don't have any bags as I can never afford to go on holiday, and I am too old and senile to be wanted by the army now, as incompetent elderly people giving out orders became unpopular after World War I.

Bob

Dear Yazz,

Re: The Only Way Is Up

I was sorry to hear on Wave 105.2FM this morning that you appear to have fallen upon hard times and sincerely hope that I am able to be of some little assistance, both in an advisory and nutritional capacity.

On the minus side, unfortunately, I am unable to share your optimism pertaining to the ease with which you may locate to alternative lodging if forced to vacate your current abode. As any other keen viewer of Can't Pay, We'll Take It Away will doubtless vouch, your intention to just move somewhere else if you should be evicted from your home may sadly not prove as straightforward as you clearly seem to anticipate, particularly if your disbarment is a corollary of rental or mortgage arrears. The moral fibre associated with one so resiliently eager to unseat themselves on the grounds of devoted emancipation is not an attribute to be insouciantly pooh-poohed. That said, Yazz, to 'Stand Up For Your Love Rights' in a hearing focussed upon a tenancy agreement breaching or defaulting resident is, I fear, unlikely to deter any presiding magistrate from applying a County Court Judgement or deciding it to be 'A Fine Time', culminating in bad references which could significantly hamper the securing of substitute accommodation.

With regard to your nescient and commiserable bewailment concerning your lamentable ignorance of where your next meal is coming from, however, my wife Jean may be able to assist. Although we may not 'have a hot one for you', if you do not mind taking pot luck, there is in the fridge, if you will pardon the pun, a 'Cold Cut' of gammon left over from last weekend's Sunday joint that we were only going to chuck out tomorrow. If you really are that hungry we are quite happy to 'hold on' if it 'won't be long'; you would be most welcome to it if you do not mind picking it up and promise to bring the Tupperware back afterwards.

We hope that we have been of some assistance and, in conclusion, respectfully confide that, in recognition of your ascent exclusivity view, we think it best that you never consider a career change from pop star to any of the following occupations:

- lift operator
- miner
- commercial pilot
- bungee jump instructor
- lumberjack
- deep sea diver
- scaffolder
- multi-storey window cleaner
- 'experience day' hot air balloonist
- tower crane driver
- archaeologist
- grave digger
- truffle locator
- forklift truck operator
- paratrooper
- Olympic ski jumper
- submarine crew member
- Eiffel Tower tour guide
- acrobatic trampolinist
- steeplejack
- stairlift installer
- trapeze artist
- juggler
- mountaineer
- independent financial adviser
- stockbroker

We would be grateful if you could also please forward this advice on to your synthetic compound community.

Yours,

Derek Philpott

PS With regard to your potential housing quandary and if you are not objectionable to the idea that you have 'got to share', it may be worth getting in touch with Heaven 17 (Official) on the popular networking website Facebook, as I understand that they are currently looking for someone to come live with them.

Dear Derek,

Mmm, firstly apologies for the delay in reply.

I just knew, however, that you would hold on, oh, I repeat hold on long enough to receive a reply to your considered opinion of my career and its possible change of profession. Life can be hard and bring with it its bottom lines and can often leave us feeling broken down on occasions. However... I find myself repeating these two words that have come to mean so much to me... hold on, Yazz, hold on to your singing career, love. As much as I do not wish to appear remotely inconsiderate or unappreciative towards the occupation of lift operator or even a pilot, in fact my mind runs riot thinking about pilots in uniforms right by my side as we'd soar to the clouds, upwards (well that would be the only way and direction you would want to be flying now, wouldn't it!).

I must also confess that I have never given much thought to a miner's life either. Not that it's artificial in any way or plastic like vinyl, certainly not, but it's just that a life underground is not for me; I prefer to work among the many inhabitants above ground level hovering somewhere between the moon and the stars!

So, boyz, I want to thank you for loving me this way in taking the time to connect and show concern for what you think is best for me as I reach for the higher heights in my career!

Sent from my basin whilst washing in a few nice L'Oreal blonde highlights!

Yazz x

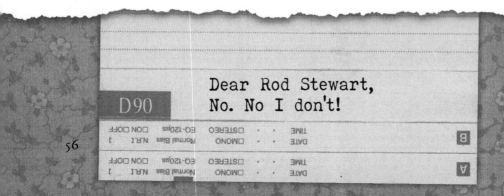

Dear Rod Stewart,
No. No I don't!

Dear 10cc,
I have no idea how a picture of me has come
into your possession and am displeased that
you are using it to cover a 'nasty stain' of
thankfully unknown origin. I must therefore
insist that the photographic image be removed
and disposed of, and recommend that the
offending discolouration be either treated,
painted (Dulux match pots are particularly
effective) or wallpapered over. Not only is the
current situation disturbing to me personally,
but it also displays a slovenly attitude to
household maintenance.

Dear Captain Sensible,

As recently explained to another pop star, I was in my younger days compulsorily enlisted into National Service in Singapore prior to my apprenticeship as a proofer. My immediate overseer, Sergeant Barraclough was, very much like yourself, Captain Sensible (in nomenclature at least), a very careful commissioning officer and, also like yourself, if one of your 'solo hits' is anything to go by, somewhat hard of hearing.

My balanced commander's partial deafness, however, was the result of a perforated eardrum sustained whilst seeing action in Sudan in 1943, as opposed to exposure to his own over-amplified 'punk rock music' at numerous 'gigs'.

Furthermore, if an address would ever be directed to what he fondly referred to as his 'wrong side' the prudent superior would respond, accompanied by way of a pained expression and jabbed finger to his left lobe, with a polite request for the comment or enquiry to be repeated into the other side of his head, after which he would normally be happy to talk. The manner of the verbal appeal would vary between 'Pardon?', 'Excuse me?', 'Sorry but I didn't quite catch that,

Private', and 'Come on now sunshine, you know that lughole is a waste of time'. Upon no occasion that I said 'Sergeant', did he say 'What?', or when I said 'Sergeant', 'What do you want?' With the passage of time, I am quite certain that, subliminally or otherwise, the reasoned disciplinarian's eloquence, as befitting his public school education, was instrumental in nurturing respect throughout the entire ranks of 85 Survey Squadron.

In order to earn similar kudos amongst your 'following' therefore, my advice to you, Captain Sensible, and indeed all other pragmatic four-stripers, is to take a leaf out of our own judicious authority figure's book and refrain from monosyllabic or brusque retorts on all future 'novelty releases'.

Yours,

Derek Philpott

....

Dear Derek,

Wot! Yes… It's a trifle repetitive, Derek, but I am in fact attempting to sing in character – as the 'pile-driver man'… the one with the extremely noisy contraption that wakes me up at some ungodly hour in a hotel mid-tour.

And I had a hangover too.

So the lyric is actually me telling a true story… (apart from the bit I chucked in about ol' Adam Wotshisname)… so true in fact is it that the VERY NOISE that awoke me that morning is the one I captured on my recording cassette Walkman and starts the splendid song we are waffling on about here.

Pip pip!

Captain Sensible

Dear 'Stiff Little Fingers',

Re: Gotta Gettaway

You have my sympathy, sirs.

I too occasionally suffer not inconsiderable discomfort directly attributable to rheumatoid arthritis, but, unlike your good selves, tend to get it not in miniature extremity digits but in my knees. Fortunately, I find that the application of a bespoke 'memory pillow' helps considerably. Occasionally, however, when I am merely mildly irritated on account of a less inflammatory joint and not in need of such bulky cushioning armamentarium, I have been known to grab it and change it for an alternative bolster, such as a pair of woollen socks or a folded tea towel.

As you are no doubt aware, it is always worse in the damp, hence, hailing as you do from Belfast, I can fully understand why you feel that you 'gotta (gotta, gotta) get away', most likely to warmer climes for a small break, in order to decrease the effects of an attack or alleviate one altogether.

I am, however, somewhat befuddled with regard to other motivations behind your yearning to go on holiday, not least your obvious irritation at clan-based coercions. Although not for one moment doubting that there may well be 'plenty of folk to tell you what to do' in your locality, I find it hard to fathom how you may interpret their discourse as of a browbeating nature when, by your own admission, 'they don't speak the same language as you'. Prior to checking flight availability on Ryanair therefore, I must recommend that on the next occasion that you witness an approaching multitude, you either refer to a phrasebook or ideally politely request the suspected scalding throng to speak clearly into your iPhone, whereupon the mass gobbledegook can be simply decoded via the Google translate 'app', thereby rendering your conjecture either substantiated or fallible and possibly avoiding unnecessary travelling expenses.

My wife Jean has also just advised me from the kitchen that our next-door but one neighbour Gordon Gillard swears by cod liver oil, and that if you have not already attempted said supplement you really should 'Go For It', given that even if the capsules do not work, you can buy a 170 ml bottle of Seven Seas Original in our area from Jolon's Pharmacy, Tuckton Road, for as little as £3.48. Even should the remedy prove ineffective, she reasons that divided four ways between 'Guitar and Drum', 87 pence is surely not 'At The Edge' of your pop star budgets these days.

We await your response at your earliest convenience, and would advise that it should not be typed out on a 'Suspect Device'; my erstwhile work colleague Willy 'Won't He' Wallace recently bought a ridiculously reasonably-priced 'Samson Galaxy' from a local car boot sale and the screen almost always 'freezes' before he can get to 'Yours faithfully'.

Yours faithfully,

Derek Philpott

....

Dear Derek,

Thanks very much for your letter. I'm very sorry to hear of your arthritic knees, it must be very painful and inconvenient when winter rolls around. I fear I must admit to being a bit of a charlatan in the arthritic finger department as the band's name is just that: a name. None of us suffer from stiffness of the digits, small or otherwise. However, your advice on the Seven Seas Cod Liver Oil is most welcome as I'm sure it brings many benefits apart from the obvious 'oiling of joints'.

As to your other advice on the unintelligibility of my countrymen, the use of a mobile phone wasn't possible when we wrote that particular song as they weren't invented at that time. However, to tie two of your threads together, I have since moved away from Northern

Ireland and now live in Chicago in the United States. Also, I am in possession of a mobile device such as you mentioned. Now, I come to a problem which pertains to a lot of what you said. This mobile phone (in fact, the very Samson Galaxy that your neighbor but one has such trouble with) seems to only recognize American accents. Therefore, when I ask it to perform even the most basic of tele-communication tasks, it singularly fails to recognize my soft, some would say 'lilting', Belfast tones. As a consequence, when I want to call a friend to arrange a night out for example, I find myself talking to the very nice Chinese gentleman who runs our local takeaway. Now, Mr Lee is a fine man and his food is delicious but he's not the guy I was hoping to discuss world affairs, sporting achievement and the market price of salmon with over a beer or two. (The price of fresh salmon is scandalous, by the way.) Sorry, I seem to have strayed from the point somewhat. Where was I? Oh yes, the transla-tion function on the phone. So, as you can see, this function almost certainly wouldn't work in my case as the phone finds it impossible to decipher my own native tongue, let alone that of anyone else I may wish to communicate with. Therefore, I am left with the origi-nal option of 'getting away'. Also, I find it's lovely to see other places, particularly in summer. Don't you?

I hope this goes some way to clearing your confusion.

Send my best to Jean and I hope you have an arthritis-free winter.

Yours faithfully,

Jake Burns

Dear Haysi Fantayzee,

Re: John Wayne Is Big Leggy

Although a cursory 'surf' of the Internet Movie Database clearly reveals the subject of your work to have been 6' 4" before he died, there is no reference whatsoever to his lower limbs being disproportionate to the rest of his body. The premise of the piece is therefore groundless. Please bear this in mind before 'penning' any more cod-rockabilly 'tunes' pertaining to the abnormal biological structures of mid-20th century western film actors. May I also suggest that clarity would be better served by eliminating toddler-speak from your future titles.

Yours,

Wilf Turnbull

....

Dear Wilf,

Thanks for the advice, Wilf. Under your tutelage I've written this new song.

Wilf Turnbull music school/
A girl can learn a lot from u/
Like what to do and what not to/
And how a song must always be true/
He knows just what will make a hit/
And without his help my songs are shit/
Unfortunately as I'm a fool/
I didn't get into Wilf Turnbull school/
And now my songs r ridiculed/ But at least the royalties pay for food/
Gaga goo goo Ga ga goo/ So I guess what I owe to u/
Is the success that comes from not following rules/

Love *Haysikate*

```
DEAR JOE JACKSON,
I WAS APPALLED TO LEARN TODAY OF PRETTY
WOMEN OUT WALKING WITH GORILLAS DOWN YOUR
STREET. NOT ONLY ARE SAID HERBIVOROUS
APES ENDANGERED, BUT THEIR INTERACTION
WITH ATTRACTIVE YOUNG FEMALES IN SUBURBAN
AREAS IS, AT BEST, UNPREDICTABLE.

DEAR JANET JACKSON,
RE: WHAT HAVE YOU DONE FOR ME LATELY?
CONSIDERING THAT I AM NEITHER IN YOUR
EMPLOY NOR ACQUAINTED WITH YOU BY BLOOD
OR THROUGH COMPANIONSHIP, PLEASE EXCUSE
ME FOR STATING THAT I FIND YOUR QUESTION
RATHER FLIPPANT. I BID YOU GOOD DAY!
```

Dear Tasmin Archer,

Re: Sleeping Satellite

In order to encourage my wife Jean to bake something other than an admittedly proficient and delicious yet ultimately monotonous Victoria Sponge as the routine denouement to our bi-Sunday roast, I decided on Tuesday to consider investing in a 'Sky package', in order that I may subtly draw her viewing attention to Ace of Cakes on The Good Food Channel and introduce a hitherto absent element of variety into her homemade 'afters' repertoire. It was whilst 'Ask Jeevesing' for a suitable outdoor antenna that the 'virtual butler' made me aware of your 1992 chart-topper and its unstable-computer-chair-featuring 'promotional video'.

I am somewhat affronted by your personal admonishments, Ms Archer, first and foremost that you blame me for the moonlit sky and the dream that died with the Eagle's flight. I think you will find that it is the sun and not I that should be censured, or, if you will pardon the pun, scalded, for fluorescing the lunar surface which in turn reflects said third party high temperature plasma-induced illumination into our nocturnal upper atmosphere, and I can assure you that I had no part in the coaching of or qualification loophole which did indeed permit the far-sighted Winter Olympian to dash our nation's hopes of a medal in the Calgary 'games' of 1988 by dint of his last placement in both the 70 and 90 metres ski-jump events.

I think you will also find that celestial bodies or objects launched into space to circumnavigate the earth or any other space-dwelling mass are not imbued with consciousness and are therefore incapable of being prone to exhaustion or drowsiness, therefore it is not possible for them to doze off. If, however, your employment of the word 'satellite' is to be interpreted in the context of a nation politically and/or economically governed by that of a more dominant neighbouring community or an interacting people located in close proximity to a large city, I will concede that a simultaneous and wholly collective nap is a conceivable if practically unenforceable scenario, but not one to which I would have any intention of apportioning irrational condemnation.

Overall I find your jaunty 'pop tune' to be not displeasing to the ear, and it has not gone unnoted that you may be related to my favourite middle-class farmers and peach-based aperitif distillers, but I will thank you to desist from penning any further odes to forty-winking implausibilities.

Yours sincerely,

Derek Philpott

Dear Derek,

Thank you for your letter. I'm very disappointed to hear that you refuse to accept any responsibility for the accusations I have made. The evidence that you are indeed culpable is beyond question and by seeking to invest in a 'Sky package' you have been hoisted by your own petard.

The last time I looked the moon was in the sky and consequently, to avoid any trade description problems, must surely be a part of any 'Sky package' which is offered for investment. Since you are a potential investor it is clear that the goal of capturing your custom has driven the vendors of said package to maintain its availability and thus the presence of the moon has been perpetuated. I suggest therefore that you are indeed to blame, in part if not wholly, for the moonlit sky.

On the second point of liability the Eagle I referenced is obviously not the 'far-sighted Winter Olympian' that you pretend to assume it is and I am not fooled for one minute by your diversionary tactics in an attempt to further deflect the first accusation. However, I was intrigued by your denial in this regard and on further investigation it appears that the Eagle you refer to was starved of investment in his preparation for the Calgary Winter Olympics. It is clear that if you had chosen to support this poor fellow financially instead of saving your pension for future investment in a 'Sky package' we all may not have had to suffer yet another national sporting disappointment. I hope you are proud of yourself.

Despite your spectacularly poor decisions as a consumer and your cunning attempts to wriggle out of any wrongdoing I must con-gratulate you on your ability to distinguish the difference between a non-conscious body and a sleeping one, something which I obvi-ously failed to do. Perhaps by exercising this skill as a free service to the medical profession you could atone for your past indiscretions and in such circumstances I may be prepared to withdraw the personal allegations I have made against you.

If I may take this opportunity to offer a little advice, instead of encouraging your wife to further develop her cake baking repertoire you should carefully examine the ingredients used in her standard fare. Judging by your state of mind I suspect that she is adding something rather special in an attempt to relieve the monotony of the 'routine denouement' and consequently your Sunday afternoons.

Love and peace,

Tasmin

I'm sorry, Def Leppard, but we don't have any sugar in at the moment as Jean and I are trying to shed some pounds after a particularly indulgent festive period. We've got some Canderel Artificial Sweeteners in the cupboard though that I can pour on you if you like but judging by how much you seem to enjoy running about onstage in your 'promotional videos', I'm afraid that I cannot guarantee that I can spell them out in the name of 'Love' with any degree of accuracy. To take a bottle and then shake it up or squeeze a little and then, once again, squeeze a little, will not be necessary, however, as they come in refill sachets. It does seem rather a strange request, though. Do you mind me asking what all this is about?

Dear Mr Priest,
In your 'metal classic', Exciter, you state that everything the gentleman touches fries into a crisp. I was just wondering (other than the Golden Wonder Baked Varieties) what happens if he actually touches a crisp?

Dear The Undertones,

I write with regard to your 'Perfect Cousin' always beating you at Subbuteo because he flicked the kick and you didn't know.

I am perplexed, The Undertones, given your assertion that Kevin always triumphed via a light blow without your knowledge. The implication appears to be that your opponent has used his thumb and forefinger to make direct contact with the ball rather than complying with Subbuteo rules clearly stating that these shooting digits should be placed behind one of the semi-circular-based mounted effigies representing his team, which should act as the intermediary between human and sphere.

In response I have no alternative but to enquire of you how it could suddenly have transpired that you now know that your flawless relative opponent committed this contravention, if at the time you were oblivious to it. Please also forgive my slight curtness in also stating that even if the Lilliputian soccer simulation atrocity can be proved, it is perhaps your own 'look out' for not keeping your eyes on the field of play in an unadjudicated match, and I have little sympathy for you.

Yours,

Derek Philpott

Dear Mr Philpott,

I thank you for your recent correspondence.

As co-author of My Perfect Cousin, I feel it is within my rights to endeavour to give you a fair and balanced reply.

Whilst your lack of sympathy over cousin Kevin's misuse of the Subbuteo rules is duly noted, I nevertheless congratulate you on your astute observance and assumption that my cocky blood relative did indeed commit, as we say in football parlance, 'a red card offence'.

I can, however, safely inform you that there is in fact a perfectly reasonable explanation to your query as to why I didn't notice this back then.

Basically, I was a very short-sighted young man at the time. Blind as a bat!

When me and Kevin partook in our now infamous games of table football, I in my misty myopic state was obviously visually impaired and in no condition to spot my crafty clever cousin abuse the standard 'flick to kick' method and use his aforementioned digits to his dirty (cheating) advantage.

This, I must add, was further exasperated by the dim living room light (a fly-ridden fluorescent tube that needed changing) and by my rather pathetic 'floodlight' effect of using my brother's camping torch pointing at the goals.

My cousin always won of course and finally, after suffering the ignominy and trauma of Chelsea (my team) getting thrashed 36–2 to his (Arsenal), I consequently refrained from ever playing the game again and retired my Subbuteo box to the attic where it still currently resides.

Kevin later confessed to me the underhand way in which he always walloped me and it was then and ONLY then that I secretly swore vengeance.

I can now attest that I did indeed have the last laugh as the yearly royalties from My Perfect Cousin – a number one smash hit in Azerbaijan, Samoa and the Kingdom of Tonga (to name a few) – has enabled me and my writing partner Michael Bradley to live a life of unbelievable grandiose luxury.

Cousin Kevin, meanwhile, is a lowly wretched estate agent…

Yours sincerely,

Damian O'Neill (guitar plucker)

Dear Mr. Difford,

Re: Up The Junction

Your 'kitchen sink classic' is unfortunately the only 'track' playable in our Nissan since our next door but one, Gordon Gillard, mistook '45s And Under' for a drinks coaster on a recent visit to return shears. Therefore, whilst my wife Jean and I are great admirers, grossly repeated exposures to the gritty narrative bely glaring oversights coupled with baffling Forteana, which led us to conventional science-flouting conclusions.

You are first, however, to be commended. In this day and age it is especially heartening to learn of an expectant parent whose partner is willing to face up to their responsibilities by putting in a hard day's graft without recourse to 'state handouts'. That said, there are some disconcerting elements pertaining to both the preparations for your first day at your new job and the position itself that demand sedulous analyses.

I find it quite unsettling that, your services being required on Monday, you had a bath on the Sunday, particularly in view of the fact that it had already been established in the preceding couplet that you had moved into a basement ruminating upon your engagement and stayed in by the telly despite the room being smelly. Having relocated, replete with said betrothal intention musings, to a fetid cellar, please forgive me for stating that any ablution, no matter how thorough, on the evening prior to your employment commencement, leaving you an entire night to be once again permeated by subterranean pungency, would not have set a good impression with your superior. Whilst fully sympathetic to your frugality, Jean also discreetly points out that the very fact that you have made reference to the tub cleansing, implying that it is a semelfactive event and therefore not a regular occurrence, could indicate that it is your good *self* that is the source of the rank underground fragrance. She therefore recommends more regular immersions if utility budgeting allows or, at the very least, Superdrug's Indus Malabar as a more economical alternative to Lynx Africa. On the other hand, it strikes her that nearly half a day of 'coming in handy', presumably via manual blue-collar exertions in keeping with your social station, would likely cancel out the effects of a good soak, and that 'Stanley', if similarly perspiring and grime-ingrained, would not be likely to 'Spot The Difference'.

As a cautionary aside, it is to be recommended that your contractual terms be rigorously scrutinised, Mr. Difford. Department of Trade and Industry Guidelines to Working Time Regulations clearly state that a toiler is entitled to an uninterrupted break of 20 minutes when daily working time is more than six hours, hence the consecutive 11 hour shift referred to is in direct contravention to the Act. Also, if, as I suspect, remuneration is of a casual 'cash in hand' variety, please ensure that all income less deductible expenses is declared on a Self Assessment Tax Return before the 31st January deadline. Failure to do so could lead to prosecution, and in extreme cases, prison. I have it on good authority from my erstwhile foreman Willy 'Won't He' Wallace, whose son was caught 'liberating' copper from some railway lines some years ago, that this is not 'Some Fantastic Place', especially at a time that your television has had to be sold and your meditative fiancée has little kicks inside her.

Finally, in relation to your occupation and salary, rather than putting away a tenner each week to improve your partner's disposition, the simple setting up of a £40 per month Standing Order, thus eradicating time-consuming trips to the bank and worries relating to burglary, fire or flooding at your dank home, could prove far more beneficial.

From hereon in, Mr. Difford, I hope you will forgive my sceptical bafflement, firstly concerning your claim to have taken her to an incubator at ten to five this morning where thirty minutes later she gave birth to a daughter. Although by no means experts in medical matters, Jean and I often watch Holby City when there is nothing else on and are quite confident that the aspirant mother would surely be ushered to the Maternity Ward upon her arrival at hospital. Said thermostat box would only be employed if complications arose after labour, and would house the infant and not the parent, who would in any case be too big to fit in it, irrespective of 'dress size'.

We are then expected to believe that your walking daughter is two years older and her mother is with a soldier. Whilst the alcohol dependency sparked estrangement and her conscriptee concord need not be debated, that your offspring could have aged 730 days since dawn, must.

I am afraid, Mr. Difford, that the only logical conclusion to be drawn from this chronological acceleration is that you are currently residing within a rip in the space/time continuum. This theory would fully explain why solid objects appear to be disappearing from your kitchen; alone there you feel there's something missing when in fact they have been removed at some point in the past. It would also solve The Mystery Of The Railway Arms, the most likely explanation being that, rather than having been lost track of, the tavern has been demolished and you are now viewing its 'vanished' aftermath from a future vantage point.

Sadly your non-Christian chauffeuring from bar to street to bookie hints at a fiendish source of this Torchwood-like phenomenon.

I strongly exhort you therefore to move *Down* The Junction as soon as possible, and most certainly not attempt to mimic your former 'boogie woogie' work colleague's BBC Two successes. 'Later… With Chris Difford', whilst still in the vortex, is likely to create severe problems with their innovative and splendid 'catch up option'.

Yours,

Derek Philpott

....

Dear Mr Philpott,

Well, what can I say? You really pushed the boat out and devoured my lyric with a fine tooth; you came, you read, you polished me off like some old red wine from a service station on the A23. For old timers you seem to know your onions, you have a great way with words, and if words were cake you would be a fine cake indeed.

I congratulate you on what you have unearthed from my lyric. Thank you. Now take the rest of the summer off and feed your goats. Life is like a pancake – you flip it and hope to catch it as it comes back down towards the frying pan. You have tossed it up and it's in mid-air, I'm standing by with the pan. But should I catch it or knock you over the head with it? Once I sang the song on stage and someone in the audience made various comments about the lyric. He and you are observers of the refined word and, my job is simply to sharpen my pencil, think of a nice place in my head and go there. What I find I never know, and often my facts are sheltered by reality. I love that in my life reality and head in the clouds are the very same thing.

I love it up here and from here I can see you on the beach in your hats, ears pressed to the glass of the radio waiting for the next song to harpoon with wonderful wit and wonder…

Many thanks,

Chris Difford (of old)

Dear Smokie,

As you are probably aware, my smouldering substance gas-originated chums, the 1970s and its accomplice the early 1980s is currently being investigated in connection to allegations of 'historical offences' as yet not focused upon Agadoo.

Therefore, and although attitudes towards accepted social decorum are admittedly 'Changing All The Time', Smokie, it is hoped that you will 'Take A Minute' to contemplate the points raised within this missive and 'Pass It Around'.

One finds it a little alarming, for example, that you should indulge in potentially inappropriate behaviour with a 'Mexican Girl' by way of perilously unacknowledging the possible hazards intrinsic to disregarding the language barrier between yourselves. So as not to have to 'Light A Candle', I recently telephoned my, if you will pardon the pun, 'current' energy supplier, requesting that my payments, based on estimated readings, be switched to reflect actual usage. After a wait of fifteen minutes even though my call was important to them, I was then told in a very cheery tone by my 'customer service representative', an otherwise delightful Newcastlian named Emily, that I was actually in arrears in the sum of £360.71. I am therefore on very 'Solid Ground', Smokie, in attesting that it is perfectly feasible for distressing news to be articulated by way of a beguiling enchantment. Ergo, it was most fortunate in your own case that, oblivious to her statement, and when you didn't know what it meant but it sounded so good that you kissed her, the consenting young lady – as opposed to would-be defendant, Juanita – was in actuality bidding you a fond Spanish farewell, and that 'hasta la vista' did not literally translate as: 'I think you are an OK bloke, but I strongly object to the concept of any physical contact with you whatsoever, Mr England Music Man, and if you insist upon advancing upon me in any way I will have no hesitation in calling the Policía Federal Preventiva.'

Similarly, your admission to be 'out cruising' when you witnessed Carol walking your way, and then pulling over, could be misconstrued by a presiding magistrate, as could Alice evacuating an adjacent property without notice after nigh on a quarter of a century without leaving either an explanation for her prompt departure or a forwarding address.

I sincerely hope that you do not mind my bringing these probable misinterpretations to your attention, sirs, and recommending that, until Scotland Yard pick on the next couple of decades, you refrain from meeting anyone at midnight unless under formal supervision.

I remain yours sincerely,

Derek Philpott

PS Jean has shouted from the kitchen (where she is making bacon sandwiches) that in light of the smoking ban and current trends you might be better renaming yourselves 'Vapie'!

....

Dear Mr Philpott,

I am bemused at your request for a discontinuation of the ancient practice of Smokeying. My ancestors have enjoyed huddling round a warm cassette machine while rhythmically moving to the sounds of those well-loved three chords and their offspring – the fourth one. You mention the 1970s as being something we should all remember, while it's a well known fact that if you remember this period you probably weren't there at all.

We did, of course, have a little trouble with spelling at school and were sent to the back of the class by a certain Mr Robinson who felt, annoyingly, that he alone had the right to dictate the spelling of what became frequently the name of a pet dog or cat. It's a miracle we ever graduated at all and I can never again look at a jar of jam without

thinking about how much of a dent Mr Robinson has made in our collective egos by insisting that we change our name to Smokie.

However, it seems that no harm was done and it took no more than a little effort to alter the spellings of all those pets' names by deed poll (particularly the ones who remained on the electoral register).

In answer to the charges contained in your missive I defend myself by saying that the Mexican Girl in question turned out to be an undercover cop who was writing a thesis on prostitution. I wouldn't normally succumb to the wiles of a dusky temptress but she was rather special (branch). We finally revealed her true intentions when, on entering her love nest, we found only photos of Arnold Schwarzenegger looking menacing and holding what looked like a cannon.

I wish for this, and several other offences involving girls whose names range from Alice to Zara (in other words the whole alphabet), to be taken into consideration and wish to be only ever, from this moment on, associated with Miss Piggy, who was my only true love right from the start.

Of course, the whole mess could have been avoided if they thought they knew how to love me, but it turned out that 'love sometimes takes time'. I don't wish to spend the whole of the rest of my career 'chasing shadows' and, after all, you 'can't change the past'.

But forty years of flying the flag of true romance can take its toll and there are parts of me (my favourite bits) that refuse to acknowledge quite so readily the advances of those 'strangers in paradise'. It is true that 'love hurts' and now we have special creams to deal with such discomforts.

Where it was once 'naked love' it is more likely quite a bit of liking coupled with a strong desire to switch off the light in order to properly view the backlit Kindle and crawl into a good book (once the late night milky drink has started to properly take effect).

Yes, even though the 1970s seem like yesterday there is strong evidence that Old Father Time has played his tricks on us and caused hair to grow in places where once we didn't even have places.

Throughout this, my testimony, I have protested my innocence and I ask your forgiveness for leading Smokie into all sorts of territories with my powerful intros, and then shepherding them off again with the corresponding outros.

I apologise to all the girls whose names did not appear on our records and ask that the 'F' word be allowed to appear in documents only when reference is made to our beloved Alice.

With thanks for your understanding.

Yours sincerely, if a little worryingly,

Martin Bullard
Smokie's Keyboard Player 1988 to 2025 (yes, I have seen a fortune teller)

PS Are you maybe related to Trevor of The Philpott File? If so, please ignore everything I have said above.

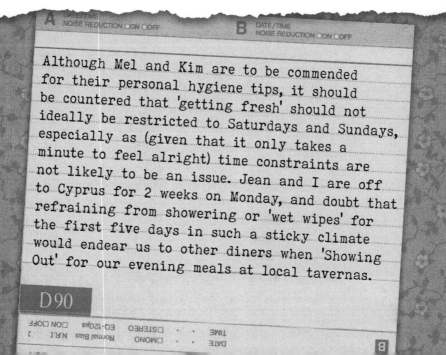

Although Mel and Kim are to be commended for their personal hygiene tips, it should be countered that 'getting fresh' should not ideally be restricted to Saturdays and Sundays, especially as (given that it only takes a minute to feel alright) time constraints are not likely to be an issue. Jean and I are off to Cyprus for 2 weeks on Monday, and doubt that refraining from showering or 'wet wipes' for the first five days in such a sticky climate would endear us to other diners when 'Showing Out' for our evening meals at local tavernas.

Dear Ms Jett,
I too am a big fan of 12 bar blues but I
resent your insistence that I should use my
own money in order to keep you entertained.
I would politely remind you that my wife
and I are pensioners, whereas you, young
lady, are a successful pop star and can well
afford to cover this cost yourself. I bid you
good day, madam!

Dear Level 42,

Re: Lessons In Love

My neighbour Wilf Turnbull and I heard your tuneful jingle on Bournemouth's Wave FM yesterday and felt compelled to congratulate you on the novel medium, that of the pop charts, through which you have chosen to promote your new enterprise. If we have one criticism, Level 42, it is that we feel that your advertising slogan, 'Could Be Better, Should Be Better', highlighting as it does the shortfalls of The Academy, is perhaps not such a good idea.

Would this be an accredited course, endorsed by 'City and Guilds'? We, together with our wives Jean and Olive, are intrigued and imagine that, if your dexterity on your musical instruments is anything to go by, one would have to be extremely proficient to attain a 'Level 42' qualification! We equally feel that the syllabus could be beneficially reciprocal given that in another of your 'jazz funk classics', The Chinese Way, you are interested in determining who knows what they know. A simple 'General Knowledge Test' aimed specifically at any students of this particular diaspora and perhaps adjudicated through an interpreter should, if marked indiscriminately, reveal the answer as your own good selves.

Jean and Olive are keen for us to scrutinise any supporting literature that you may have, with a view to Wilf and myself considering possible enrolment when the course has been improved, if we feel the tutelage fees and related costs to be reasonable. Please be advised that we must politely decline any 'freshening up' facilities that may be available 'on campus', as it appears that you may have a malfunctioning thermostat. Until such time as this may be repaired, for baths or showers that may be running *for* the family, and to avoid sons and daughters in hot water in future, may I recommend the 'elbow test', which both children and adults say ensures that water temperature is optimum and avoids juvenile or infant scalding.

Yours,

Derek Philpott (with help from neighbour Wilf)

....

Hello Derek and Wilf,

In reply to your insightful letter to us, I have to hold my hands up and say you are quite right. The Academy is rubbish, sorry.

If we could do better we undoubtedly would, but there it is…!

Re The Chinese Way, and 'who knows what they know?', well it is actually Hoonose Watheyno, a legendary Chinese person whose legend just keeps growing. Exponentially.

Re Hot Water, I've just heard back from Guy Garvey and the boys who passed it with flying colours, so no problem there either.

Have a lovely Christmas, or Easter if you are reading this in three months' time.

Mx
Mark
www.level42.com

Dear Mr. Fish,

I am a little perplexed, Mr Fish, by your assertion that we are (presumably you are referring to our good selves perhaps in addition to hitherto unknown third parties) just sugar mice in the rain.

I hope you will also forgive me for stating that the very employment of the word 'just' as an adverb grossly understates the gravity of such a human to soaked carbohydrate murine transformation.

Not only is it currently quite sunny outside at the moment but, aside from a few whiskers that I decided to cultivate to commemorate a particularly successful 'Movember', I do not appear to resemble a small saccharine rodent, sodden or otherwise, in the slightest at the time of writing.

As regards your request that I blame this currently unrealised predicament on you, considering that to the best of my knowledge we have never met, I find it difficult to fathom how you could be held accountable for any metamorphosis into a precipitation-soaked diminutive confectionery mammal that I may be yet to undergo.

Furthermore, given that I am several years your senior and am fully aware that my father Ernest was not Scottish, there is no feasible way in which you could be my 'Daddy', thus your taking of a raincheck is immaterial.

Might I suggest as an aside that many other 'pick and mix staples' such as cola bottles, pear drops, 'gummy' bears and worms, jelly babies/beans, shrimps, fizzy dummies and 'chews' may prove more resilient in a downpour, for your future reference.

Yours,

Derek Philpott

Dear Mr Filluppot,

While in a meditative trance in the late 80s in a Peruvian burial chamber assisted by Mayan brethren and under the influence of some right wicked rainforest shrooms I had a vision in which you came to me dressed as a mousey Barbara Cartland all in pink like and with righteous whiskers and such. A long rather fetching string tail fed from your evening gown and you were squeaking but in the Queen's English. You kept on repeating results from the Vauxhall Conference League and bus timetables from Milwaukee as well as occasionally singing Sinatra songs in Yiddish!

I took this as a sign and knew that the great god Tumultacan wished me to convey to the human race their oncoming demise. Your appearance as a pink saccharine rodent deity in my trance in the confines of the rainforest where humidity levels reach dangerous levels was a message that the great rapture was upon us.

Despite human attempts to burn the said rainforests down to alleviate the danger the raingods have been sweeping the world with downpours and flooding as they assumed that the vision I had of you suggested a further evolutionary process where the human race, which they consider vermin, were in fact susceptible to melting under mass precipitation as they mutated into pastel coloured sweeties.

I awoke from my trance in a rather tepid bath in Aylesbury and felt a compulsion to warn the world and wrote the lyric in fountain pen in Sanskrit on rather soggy blotting paper where the warning was lost in translation and transcription by my former band mates who found me later suffering from exposure and deep 3rd degree wrinkling. Desperately in need of a missing lyric, they rushed the creation through and after I came out of the unit they'd put me in for a few months I was forced to sing at gunpoint words which I had never intended, the original warning I wanted to proclaim censored by the record company as they were scared it would damage worldwide sales.

My prophecy of the watery demise of the human race is now proving to be true and I urge you to check your backside in the bathroom mirror every day for any emergence of string and to lick the palms of your hands regularly for any signs of sugary crystallisation. I perform this ritual regularly.

You were meant to write this letter to me for I know it was part of the prophecy and you now have to fulfil your own destiny.

Now stop what you are doing, put on that pink Barbara Cartland gown that I know is in your wardrobe and go into the streets and squeak to the world!

I am your daddy!

Love,

Fish

PS Take an umbrella

Bryan Adams has stated that everything he does, he does for me. The soft-rocker recently visited the Canadian Prime Minister and had his photograph taken with him. He also performed at the opening ceremony of the International Cricket Council's World Cup tournament in Bangladesh. I can categorically state that neither action benefited me in any way, shape or form whatsoever. I bid him good day!

Dear Mr Dean Taylor,
I am sorry to hear there is a ghost in your house, and do not envy you the likely months of legal wrangling ahead and being on hold for twenty minutes at a time as you attempt to argue with the Local Authority that you actually are still technically entitled to a single person's occupancy discount in relation to your council tax.

Dear Mr Wonder,
I write with no little urgency. Neither Jean nor I recall ordering a Motown singer and are thus very anxious at your claim to be signed, sealed, delivered and ours. Notwithstanding the fact that neither of us have scrawled an indecipherable signature on a slippery screen, you are yet to arrive and are probably at the sorting office. We sincerely hope that your packaging allows for sufficient air holes and are also quite alarmed that Royal Mail have permitted such a live cargo.

Dear The Communards,

Re: Never Can Say Goodbye

You have my heartfelt condolences, The Communards. I learnt of your leave-taking disorder on Radio Two this morning and was both discombobulated and dismayed to hear that you never can say goodbye, especially as prior to the Ken Bruce-induced divulgation I was incognisant of such an unfortunate farewell articulation-based allergic malady.

Being by no means an expert on such afflictions, I can thus only imagine the umpteen hardships affiliated to an adieu-bidding repellency and must only hope that you have formulated a universally recognised etymological alternative to précising interminable meandering conversations at social functions and business meetings, and selected a premium mobile handset tariff that comes with an abundance of free minutes. Sadly, however, your disclosure that you suffer a same old dizzy hang up suggests an inveterate disequilibrium symptomatic of finally concluding a phone call devoid of a truncating valediction, resulting in recurrent giddiness.

It is therefore completely understandable that, as confessed in another of your '80s hits', you have no desire to be left this way.

I am nonetheless perplexed, The Communards, that you claim a perpetual inability to say goodbye and yet have somehow managed to achieve said 'impossible' feat no fewer than twenty one times (excluding the splendid female 'backing vocals') over the course of less than five minutes, within your pop song. Said successfully repeated parting enunciations clearly indicate one of two possible scenarios, either of which will result in the need for re-recording, I am afraid, in order to establish transparency and accuracy.

I therefore look forward to hearing the corrected adjustment, be it 'I Am Unable To Say Goodbye In Certain Situations' or 'I Never Can Actually *Say* Goodbye But I *Can* Sing It' on my Nissan's wireless in the near future.

Yours,

Derek Philpott

....

Dear Mr Philpott,

Thank you for your kind letter and may I take this opportunity of wishing you, on behalf of the Communards, a very happy new year?

As to your question, like so many other synth pop bands of the 80s, I think we were always anxious in our songs to draw a distinction between time in the sense of 'chronos' and time in the sense of 'kairos'. Thus never saying goodbye is both a single point in time/ chronos, and yet also a perpetual state of farewell-paralysis in time/ kairos. I hope this clears it up.

Yours sincerely,

Richard Coles

Dear Sailor,

We once had lunch with the captain of the Wightlink catamaran service from Portsmouth Harbour to Ryde on his day off. He was a very pleasant fellow whom we met 'Down At The Docks' before boarding, and he was very passionate about his job. Indeed, nothing could 'Stop That Man' enthusing about it, and after 'One Drink Too Many' he detailed, quite without prompting, the specifics of his not insubstantial salary.

Well knowing, therefore, that a sailor's income is quite high, and unless you are quite deliberately avoiding 'pushing the boat out', your offer of the two of us (for reasons unknown) getting together over a single glass of champagne, as opposed to a half bottle or even a glass each, is confusing.

Although the frugal singular flute sparkling beverage offer does seem to suggest that you may be struggling to make ends meet (as also evidenced by two of your members only seeming to be able to afford one piano between them), you do clearly state that 'you have the money' befitting of such lucratively paid mariners.

Assuming that 'Nothing Has Changed' in the generous remuneration of seafarers, the only possible conclusions to be drawn are sadly that you are either unable to manage your financial affairs properly or, as my father used to say of a senior work colleague who would always coincidentally disappear to the gents whenever it was his round, have 'deep pockets but short arms'.

As regards either scenario, I am a little affronted by your inaccurate disclosure that I have the figure full of delights, and your presumptuous designs upon it. I will have you know, Sailor, that I only retain a sufficiently modest balance in my Santander 1-2-3 account to cover bills and sundries, and that any disposable funds that I do ever have left over are to be enjoyed by close family and friends in preference to nautical Nickelodeon specialists.

In any event, I am afraid that I would object to drinking out of the same glass as your good selves, simply because I was once asked on the terraces by my friend Tony Beasley to sip his oxtail Cup-a-Soup because he thought it tasted funny when, unbeknownst to me, he was going down with a bug.

If you *are* genuinely 'Out Of Money', shipmates, may I recommend that you try and scrape together at least one extra glass and add a touch of Tesco Value lemonade to a bottle of Blue Nun, and perhaps adopt a less misleading monicker more befitting of your reduced circumstances, such as, perhaps 'Canoeist' or 'Pedalo Steerer'.

I remain yours sincerely,

Derek Philpott

....

Dear Mr Philpott,

Your reputation has gone before you for many more years than you can possibly imagine.

Prior to what my doughty maritime colleagues and I considered a measured and reasonable invitation to your good self to join us for an evening of jovial banter that would involve a degree of ethanolic consumption, we were distressed to discover that we were to spend a considerable amount of time with one Derek – fill pot – Philpott; a man renowned for his ability to fill and, more to the point, empty flagon after flagon of the most expensive examples of the vintners' art.

As a result, we felt obliged to, somehow, limit the supply of aperitifs (and split infinitives) available to your good self on your arrival at my place.

As well as the place, we had the money to indulge you to the degree stated. In fact, we were prepared to extend the invitation as far as the five of us over five glasses of Bollinger's best vintage.

Sadly, on your arrival, we were distraught to discover that you neither had the figure nor the face.

Furthermore, even though we had provided the music and the lights it was evident that your figure was far from full of delights.

I do concede that, in your view, I may have neither position nor name, but your claim to have the power to drive me insane was, to put it mildly, an overstatement.

In view of the above issues, I feel that I was entitled to limit my offer to only one glass of the Heidsieck or Moët between us.

Yours faithfully,

Grant Serpell

Dear Mr Lemmy,
With the possible exception of, arguably, Snap and, as admittedly important and symbolic as the playing card under scrutiny is undoubtedly considered to be, I think you will find that the ace of spades held in isolation is an ineffective proposition pertaining to securing victory in many of today's recognised games, requiring as it does, to be, for example, part of a flush or four of a kind. If, however, I am mistaken and you are in fact referring to holding, for example, 3 of a kind, and are disclosing your predicament to fellow competitors that the ace of spades is the only card you need, I suggest that this is perhaps not the best course of action to take, and must therefore strongly recommend that you refrain from casinos and/or 888 Online Poker until your strategy has been adjusted.

Dear Dean Friedman,

Re: Lydia

I was genuinely moved whilst listening to your heartfelt ballad on my iPod Walkman today, Mr Friedman, both by its plaintive refrain and the ticket inspector who informed me that my ticket was not valid in a first class carriage.

At the risk of causing disappointment, however, it is my considered opinion that your relationship with the young lady referred to within the piece should be terminated forthwith.

You clearly croon that Lydia keeps your toothbrush in her apartment and she never, or hardly ever, complains.

Personally, I fail to see how the storage of any oral hygiene instrument could be the cause of grievance, unless:

a) the tufts are contaminated with gingivitis or rotting meal remnants (both of which can only be transmitted via insertion into a mouth alternative to that of the petite dental broom's last known owner, at the latest user's own peril and without liability to the aforementioned originator)

b) it is of the electric variety and a fault originating from the base unit housing the built-in charger now renders it a fire hazard

c) it is, unlike my own Medium Colgate Zig Zag Plus, which I have just measured at six and a quarter inches in length and would not take up too much room in any 'condo' no matter how cluttered, an extremely bulky 'novelty' specimen of the type seen wielded by Chris Evans in 'publicity stills' promoting his shaft-mounted bristles, recollection-encouraging 'game show' and thus, perhaps, an unwelcome and pointless devourer of valuable storage space

More central to my estrangement recommendation, however, is the inescapable truth that your suitor seems to have formed an unhealthy infatuation attachment towards your compact incisor scrubbing device which is currently within her possession, and is convinced that the non-sentient celluloid-stemmed synthetic fibre-implanted cleansing utensil, the handle of which she does not appear to have gripped for quite some time, is actually a young male close to passing away. This is sadly proved by her referring to it as 'Boy' and stating that she thought it was dead on account of it being so long since she had held it (itself an unorthodox parameter for gauging health, even in animate objects).

In conclusion, then, and contrary to your mournful chorus, I urge you to wrestle yourself from Lydia's command and offer her guidance as to the official channels appropriate to qualified psychiatric evaluation. I fully acknowledge that this is more than you had planned but, although you may be extremely well matched (for reasons I will address in a moment), she has clearly displayed her potential for infidelity within courtship, and hopefully the process should take its natural course. Please take great care not to disclose to any medical professional, as revealed within the rocking chair song, that you believe household furniture, radios, platforms protruding from the exteriors of buildings and crockery to be talking to you. It's not 'gonna be alright'. I hope you will forgive me for stating, Mr. Friedman, that if your lucky stars are to be thanked for anything it is your own evasion thus far from institutionalisation. You may well need a place to stay but I hope you will agree that an asylum is far from ideal under any circumstances.

I wish you all the best.

Yours,

Derek Philpott

Dear Derek Philpott,

I feel compelled to reply to your somewhat naive and clearly misinformed missive as regards my utilitarian relationship with Lydia.

Firstly, I'm dismayed by your blatantly prejudicial bent, when it comes to your unapologetic dismissal of 'so-called' inanimate or non-sentient objects. Coming, as you do, from a country that prides itself on promoting the welfare of animals, your callous lack of empathy for the feelings of household furniture and appliances is both hypocritical and disheartening.

Any person who has experienced the manifold joys of sharing their lives with that special ottoman, bolster, coffee table, or throw-rug; that faithful ladle, spatula, back-scratcher, DVD player or commode, knows beyond any shadow of a doubt that objects do, indeed, have feelings, are possessed of a unique and divine spirit, and are deserving of our utmost respect, care and consideration.

It's clear to me that you must have been severely traumatized in your youth by some wayward Murphy bed, or perhaps injured in some folding chair mishap. This saddens me greatly, as it means you have missed out on one of life's greatest joys – a loving relationship with those wonderful furnishings and appliances that share, and are, in fact, the place we call our home.

It's not too late, though, Derek. Therapy can do wonders. And are you so close-minded and arrogant as to assume that the benefits derived from time spent on an analyst's couch are solely those of the analysts? What of the couch, Derek? What of the couch?!

In closing, I'm pleased to report that a relatively inexpensive package of rechargeable lithium batteries has brought my toothbrush, still residing in Lydia's flat, 'back from the dead'. I haven't had occasion to visit Lydia in quite a while, but I know with great certainty that Lydia and my electric toothbrush – with its numerous replaceable attachments – are sharing a full, happy and productive life in a one bedroom flat in London, with, as far as I know, no complaints!

Sincerely,

Dean Friedman

Dear Gonzalez,

Although unaware of when the initial potentially romantic rendezvous occurred, I find it rather disconcerting that you haven't stopped dancing yet since you met on a first date. I am afraid that from a personal safety point of view, shaving, making hot drinks, and operating motor vehicles in your present disposition is NOT alright, alright, alright, alright.

Yours,

Derek Philpott

....

Hey Derek,

'My sweet feet can't stop the beat'.

I still sing I Haven't Stopped Dancing Yet.

In fact it has saved my life. I had a heart bypass 16 yrs ago and have been performing that song most weekends at 133 BPM.

It's the perfect heart workout.

Peace & Love,

Lenny Zakatek… Gonzalez

'NEVER FORGET WHERE YOU'VE COME HERE FROM', ADVISE TAKE THAT, WISELEY. I AM CURRENTLY AT HARRY RAMSDEN'S FISH AND CHIP RESTAURANT AND DISTINCTLY RECALL LEAVING MY HOUSE TO GET HERE. SHOULD THIS EVER CEASE TO BE THE CASE I WILL CONSULT MY GP IMMEDIATELY.

Dear The JoBoxers,

I am proud to relate, The JoBoxers, that my wife Jean and I have connections to the Dogs Trust. It was therefore with no little pride that we found ourselves in a position to help our Gala Bingo partners Nigel and Alicia Saxtonhouse in securing an adorable one-eyed terrier cross from the Newbury re-homing centre last month, who was apparently little more than 'skin and bone' when admitted some weeks previously. On the return journey, as we entered the M3 sliproad, what should come on Absolute Radio but your 'feel-good hit', which perfectly encapsulated the joyous scenario whereby we had 'Just Got Lucky'!

Slightly more perplexing, however, was your insistence on Wave 105.2FM this morning that should I be able to fulfill a list of near Herculean criteria, then I will be 'doing the Boxerbeat'.

Frankly, sirs, I hope you will excuse me confiding that, were I actually able to accomplish the monumental achievements of, amongst others, 'just' letting the crippled ones walk, the lazy ones work, the blind so they see, and the sad ones happy, I am likely to establish an autocratic regime dedicated to the enrichment of others, rather than indulge in a pugilistic pounding prioritisation.

On a completely related note one wonders if the procedure of 'letting the silent ones talk' is reversible and can be applied to many of today's current politicians.

I am also confused by your declaration that I will be syncopationally sparring after shaking my knees and planting my feet, only to be slightly later instructed to keep my feet on the loose. I am afraid, gentlemen, that this 'Don't Add Up', on the basis that their burial in soil is likely to restrict all freedom of movement.

All points considered, The JoBoxers, I hope that you will not be offended by my reluctance to go to so much effort merely to simultaneously drum and drub, or observe that your chances of World Title contendership are considerably in excess of 'One In A Million' should you restrict yourselves exclusively to accepting bouts with a Jordan, Josh, Joseph and, especially on a psychological level, find a Johnny friendly.

Yours,

Dérek Philpott

....

Dear Mr Philpott,

Thank you for your recent letter informing JoBoxers of your successful endeavour at the Dogs Trust. An adorable one-eyed terrier was quite a find to be sure, although there is no mention of said terrier specifically being a Jack Russell wearing cap and cardigan, the only breed synonymous with our song, Just Got Lucky. A one-eyed Boston Terrier, certainly a fine animal, would not qualify as the perfect encapsulation of your joyous scenario. However, as you might surmise from our band name, we are sportsmen and therefore prepared to offer you the benefit of the doubt at the close of Round 1. Points tied.

Before we discuss you, Mr Philpott, attempting to do the Boxerbeat, we must congratulate you on your excellent suggestion with regard to today's politicians. Lyrically, 'let the talkers be silent' does not flow quite as well as 'let the silent ones talk', but the idea of muzzling (to continue the animal theme) those unprincipled dogs who love to hear themselves talk and are often barking up the wrong tree, usually for their own financial gain and self-aggrandisement, definitely puts you a point up at the end of Round 2. Let us raise our collective legs on the vast majority of them.

I do realise, Mr Philpott, that Boxerbeat does ask rather a lot of one, but are we not encouraged as children to reach for the stars and as adults to succeed beyond our wildest dreams? This is a positive message and one that I suggest you put to good use, maybe as part of your morning constitutional? You may be retired, but the answer to a good long life is still a little exercise first thing in the morning. So let's start with shaking your knees, not forgetting to concentrate on a constant and affirmative mental attitude, then move on to planting your feet – please do this on a solid surface, as it's not our intention for you to become a tree. Now shuffle your feet around (keep your feet on the loose). I don't think we need to be concerned with keeping your neck from the noose, unless of course you have recently decided to dispose of one of the aforementioned unprincipled dogs. This would doubtless lead to a national manhunt and, as you'd be on the run, so to speak, make the necessity of your morning constitutional redundant. Now, back to shaking your knees. And so on... I know it's somewhat presumptuous, but Round 3 goes to JoBoxers. Total points again tied.

You are right in stating that our chances of a World Title at this late stage in the game is well beyond One In A Million; in fact, sadly, we no longer accept bouts other than this rather sedate form of competition that we are indulging in here. You will note also, Mr Philpott, from the end of the last paragraph that we are tied on points, both of us highly unlikely to have the stamina to go the full 15 rounds (the band is retired too) and would all rather opt for a trip down the pub for a pint or three. Let us know when a gathering would be convenient for you and your esteemed colleague, Mr. Turnbull – the beer is on us.

Sincerely,

Johnny Friendly aka *Dave Collard* (JoBoxers, retired)

Dear The Steve Miller Band,

I was referred to you by Top of the Pops 2, as I am looking for a close-up magician to perform at Gordon Gillard's granddaughter's wedding in November.

I have a few reservations, however, which will need to be addressed prior to making a full booking.

Firstly, given your assertion that every time I call your name you heat up like a burning flame, I was wondering if I could address you by an alternative, possibly stage, monicker (such as 'The Space Cowboy', 'Maurice' or 'The Gangster of Love', perhaps) when telephoning you to confirm parking arrangements just before the event, in order to avoid your combustion when picking up the receiver. Furthermore, after saying 'Abra-abra-cadabra', could we please have it from you in writing that you will not reach out and grab any of the guests, but instead move on to the next table to perform the next sleight of hand, as we fear that your intended over-familiarity would not be acceptable in such a formal setting.

Finally, before the booking can be finalised, some finer points regarding outfits are required to be 'ironed out'. Clarification as to who is to be bedecked in silk and satin, leather and lace, black panties with an angel face is required, owing to ambiguity within your UK Dave performance. If it is indeed to be your own stagewear, please be advised that suits, shoes and handkerchiefs tailored from the materials outlined are perfectly commendable. However, seraph-emblazoned undergarmentry, if one must, will only be acceptable if covered, preferably by a pair of smart trousers.

I need not add that should these requirements not be adhered to on the evening of the engagement in question, there will be no opportunity for you to 'take the money and run', as payment would be in the form of a stoppable cheque.

I sincerely hope that this letter reaches you right there, right there, right there, right there at home as soon as possible, in order that we may address these points and hopefully ensure that young Ellen's big day will indeed be 'Something Special'.

Yours,

Derek Philpott

....

Dear Derek,

I am not Steve Miller. Let us get that much clear immediately. I am much poorer, have far less talent, and am immensely better looking than the mysterious Mr Miller. I did, however, work with Steve as a part of his band for several years, having co-written and played guitar on his hit 'Jungle Love', the song that answers the burning question, 'What would happen if Dr. Seuss took an enormous dose of LSD?' The fact that I see Steve once a year gives me, to my sociopathic manner of thinking, complete permission to handle all his musical and personal affairs.

Mr Philpott, it is time for the Hamster of Love to re-invent himself. We accept the magic gig. 'We'. Both of us. Think of me not as a pathetic hanger-on trying desperately to curry favor with the guy who writes me enormous checks every three months but as... The

Sorcerer's Apprentice. (By the way, with a name like 'FILL-pot', you didn't have a chance, did you? You HAD to be funny. It's kind of the whole Boy-Named-Sue thing…)

Now, let's address some of your concerns. 'Every time I call your name you heat up like a burning flame'. A valid concern, since Steve is a veritable tsunami of pseudonyms. Maurice? The Gangster? Utter the wrong name and poof!, spontaneous combustion. As we all know, the sudden cremation of even a couple of guests at a party can really put a damper on things, as evidenced recently when the cousin of Steve's road manager called Steve 'Mr Space Cowboy' backstage. Flame on! Between the high-pitched screams and the awful stench, one would have thought that Journey had taken the stage.

May I suggest that everyone address Steve with the appellation 'Ed'? It's short, it's generic, and it's fireproof. Consequently, you may refer to me as 'Ed's Bitch'. No one will be burned alive, but they might receive an open-handed slap across the face.

Now… the whole black panties with an angel's face thing… actually, it should be an Angel's face capitalized, as in Hell's Angel. The Angel in question is a Russian fellow named Rip Yercockoff. He's in charge of our security and yes, he wears black panties and a leather jacket with motorcycle boots. YOU tell him he looks like Ernest Borgnine in drag. Go ahead, Derek. Once Mr Yercockoff starts in on you, you'll be screaming 'SPACE COWBOY!!!!' at Steve and praying for the sweet embrace of a quick cremation.

Finally… and I know you've thought about this many times… what IS the 'Pompitous of Love'? OK here it is, straight from the source: the Pompitous of Love is the pet name for a small, oozing sore on Mr Miller's meat thermometer that appeared shortly after he had a carnal cuddle with a woman named Penelope Pompy back in 1972. Thus, anything grotesque and sickening is said to be possessed of POMPY-tous properties.

Do not speak of the Pompitous of Love in front of security chief Yercockoff.

Please send a contract to my attention as soon as possible with dates, times, and the amount and method of payment. I'll be honest: I've been working real hard and I'm trying to find a job but it just keeps getting tougher every day. However, I know in my heart that if I do my part, the economy still blows and we will all die alone.

It's been a pleasure doing business with you.

Yours truly,

Greg Douglass

Dear Madonna,
I am confused. My next door but one neighbour, Gordon Gillard, informs me that his son Michael managed to get backstage on your 'Blond Ambition Tour' in 1990 by wearing a reflective tabard. However upon calling your name you did not say a little prayer but instead called for security who immediately had him removed from the stadium complex. Please amend the lyrics of your hit to reflect said ejection, post haste.

Dear The Talking Heads,
Forgive me for stating that burning down the house hardly constitutes the behaviour of an 'ordinary guy'. Arson is generally committed by criminals, the unstable and/or unscrupulous publicans or unsuccessful nightclub owners, in the form of what is widely termed an 'insurance job'.

I am very angry with some pop stars at the moment, very angry indeed. My son is a keen guitarist and a great fan of Mark Knopfler and his cohorts, so for his birthday I was delighted to be able to buy for him a 'backing track' CD called 'Play Guitar With Dire Straits'. Thus far, and despite numerous repeats, the band have reneged on their part of the bargain and have not arrived at the lad's house. What a misleading waste of £13.99! They really are getting money for nothing!!!

Dear Heaven 17,

Thank you for your invitation to 'Come Live With Me'. Unfortunately, Olive and I are unable to accept, as we feel that you may not have considered the full implications of such an arrangement. We both enjoy peace and quiet now and again at our age, and while we are very fond of your tuneful offerings, I fear that the constant accompaniment of 'New Wave Synth-Pop' may eventually lead to domestic discord. In addition, we already have a nice house, and have got rather used to using the bathroom and other facilities at our own pace. We would love to visit you one day, and of course you would be most welcome to pop in at Turnbull Towers. If you are looking for more permanent 'housemates', may I suggest you approach Living In A Box, who I believe are in less than satisfactory accommodation at present.

On a different note, I must congratulate you on highlighting the dangers of being 'Crushed by the Wheels of Industry'. Our neighbour Gordon Gillard has recently acquired a mobility scooter, and has been driving it in a frankly reckless manner. Olive had a narrow escape on Thursday afternoon when he almost ran over her foot on the corner of Herberton Road. I appreciate that after years of shuffling with a walking stick, the 'Temptation' of the accelerator pedal is irresistible, but he is an absolute menace to pedestrians in the Southbourne area, particularly when travelling downhill. In the interests of road safety, perhaps you could write a characteristically catchy song advising Gordon to slow down, as he does not appear to listen to me.

Best regards

Wilf Turnbull

....

Dear Wilf,

Thank you very much for your letter. I must admit, I was at first disappointed at your turning down of my offer to 'Come Live With Me' but on reflection I can see that it was perhaps a little forward and to be honest, I think a rather impractical proposal. There would of course have been 'space' issues; indeed we only have the one bathroom and I could see, even if we did have a very well worked out rota system there would still be times when needs were great and a single bathroom would not suffice. I also understand that you and Olive are happy where you are and I have no wish to put such a loving relationship under any outside pressure. (It's a well-known fact that moving house is one of the most stressful things that one can do.) I would, however, like to clear one thing up. There would not be a 'constant accompaniment' of 'New Wave Synth-Pop Music' around the house. Since building a studio at the bottom of my garden approximately 11 years ago now, all synthesizers and electronic keyboards have been stored and played within its soundproof environs, leaving the house and indeed garden a 'Synth-Pop' free zone. With regards to Living In A Box, I must admit I do feel for their situation. Homelessness is an enormous problem both here in the inner city and in rural areas but I believe in their case it is a somewhat self-inflicted dilemma and do not at this moment feel an offer to take them in would help them in the long run (I hope this doesn't seem too harsh).

Now regarding your problem with Mr Gordon Gillard. You're right to point out the dangers of these 'death machines'. The rise in use of mobility scooters is rather alarming and is exactly the kind of thing we were indeed warning against in our public information song, Crushed By The Wheels of Industry. The frankly callous and careless way some people behave once they get behind the wheel of one of these speed machines is nothing less than a national disgrace. You're right to suggest the penning of a special song highlighting the dangers of Mobility Scooter Madness. I think the title 'Slow Down Gordon' is a wonderful starting point for a new song and I can already hear in my mind's eye (can one hear in the mind's eye?) how the song should progress. Thank you, Wilf, for this new musical inspiration.

Well I had better go now but it would be nice to see you and Olive soon, even if it was just for a long weekend or perhaps over a bank holiday period.

All the best,

Glenn Gregory
Heaven 17

Dear Messrs. Sputnik,

Re: Love Missile F1-11

I am afraid, gentlemen, that you have placed me in quite a precarious position. At a family event last week attended by members that I had never met before, I was introduced for the first time to my second cousin's husband's niece, whom I established over a suspected Iceland-heavy buffet to be friendly with the former personal assistant to a retired NATO envoy. Obviously, I felt compelled to air my concerns relating to the lethal new weapon publicised by yourselves last week, which I chanced upon when logging into the Spotify jukebox and searching for the Formula One theme tune. As a keen humanitarian who prides herself on still keeping tabs on potential peacekeeping-initiative-jeopardising military developments, Ms Siddiqi was quick to express her surprise at never having heard of the concupiscent warhead to which you had referred, and commented that she found this especially confusing given that the juxtaposition of such a harmonious word with one synonymous with mass devastation presented a jarring paradox which she felt sure that she would have remembered at a Christening. She then appeared to be somewhat preoccupied during the font group photographs before leaving the place of worship at great haste, claiming an upset stomach which at the time I attributed to an only partially defrosted Chicken Zinger Slider.

I have, however, just this morning received a rather terse email from the newly baptised's father, who states that the actual motive for the ex-diplomatic delegate secretary acquaintance's sudden departure was for immediate and pressing investigatory enquiries to commence into the passionate projectile at hand, in order to proactively avert any crisis situation being considered to be instigated by an oppressive regime. Her preliminary report states that no records exist of an F1-11 model (the nearest contender being the non-ardent surface to surface Fateh-110) or, obviously when considering its unmanufactured state, any plans to 'shoot it up'. As an acerbic rejoinder, she adds that she has located your appearance on Top of the Pops which references US bombs cruising overhead, and correctly posits that said airborne munitions should hardly be a concern given the allegiance that we have to our transatlantic cousins, but that in the event of our territories ever being at variance, sanctuary best be sought in a bunker or Anderson shelter in preference to an exposed Shepherds Bush entertainment complex, and that your 'look' of large multi-coloured wigs, pink stiletto heels and distressed Satsuma bag-styled 'fright masks' should be dispensed with in favour of more sombre costuming less likely to give away your position to the enemy.

As an aside, and in relation to your insinuation that prevailing styles are accountable for an increase in juvenile misdemeanours, I must myself counter that teenage crime is more likely to be resultant of lax parenting than the arguable assertion that 'fashion's dead'.

Thanks to yourselves, Messrs Sputnik, I have now been strictly forbidden from panicking any further distant relatives cordial with previous employees of intergovernmental affiliation collectives at formal gatherings, by way of engaging them in conversational topics in any way connected to affection-generating related torpedoes, and would therefore thank you only to sing about listed armaments of yearning in the future, especially before my son's 50th.

I bid you good day!

Yours,

Derek Philpott

....

My Dear Mr Philpott,

I was most intrigued – and might I say mildly amused – by your missive of 22nd December 2013. Unfortunately I have reached the age where urgency is confined to matters of a delicate nature (hrmph) so please forgive the rather extended delay in answering.

I was most interested in the reaction, and subsequent research, of your family member Ms Siddiqi. I'm afraid the calibre of government 'intelligence' officers is sorely lacking these days. Even the most cursory glance over armaments on the internet should have flagged the F-111 Bomber as being of almost legendary status in the US Air Force. There is even a Wikipedia page on the subject: http://en.wikipedia.org/wiki/General_Dynamics_F-111_Aardvark

And here is a picture:

The fact that my former bandmates and I chose to move the hyphen to render our song title Love Missile F1-11 (largely to avoid copyright issues, and to avoid mispronunciation issues) should NOT have put off any amateur sleuth – let alone a 'pro'.

I can therefore deduce that your cousin, Ms Siddiqi, is NOT who she seems and would urge you, and your good lady wife, to be on your guard! You can't be too careful these days… Your suspicions should have been aroused by the aforementioned Ms Siddiqi claiming her illness was caused by her Chicken Zinger Slider not being fully defrosted as I'm sure you and your good lady wife would check such matters.

The 'Love' part of the song title in question refers, of course, to the exceptional film Dr Strangelove or: How I Learned to Stop Worrying and LOVE the Bomb!

And I realise of course that fashion isn't dead… It just doesn't look as if it's very well judging by the outfits sported by some of the 'modern' pop personae. Not enough originality for the 21st century to my mind… It almost looks as if all the pop stars are dressed by the same three stylists… Funny that.

Please don't be shy about writing again – Unlike Señor Luis Suarez I don't bite these days!

Kind regards,

Neal Whitmore

Formerly of Sigue Sigue Sputnik – Now fronting The 'Fabulous' Montecristos
Facebook <http://www.facebook.com/TheMontecristos>
Twitter <http://twitter.com/TheMontecristos>
Instagram <http://instagram.com/themontecristos>
General Dynamics F-111 Aardvark – Wikipedia, the free encyclopedia
en.wikipedia.org

IN HIS SONG, MR. MISTER REFERS TO TAKING BROKEN WINGS WITH A VIEW TO LEARNING TO FLY AGAIN. IT IS MY SINCERE HOPE THAT MR. MISTER IS NOT A PRACTISING VETERINARIAN GIVEN THAT HIS POP CHART DIAGNOSIS LEAVES MUCH TO BE DESIRED. ALTHOUGH NOT EXPERT IN AVIAN HEALTH MATTERS, ONE WOULD NATURALLY ASSUME THAT AN INJURED BIRD WOULD NOT BE IN NEED OF FLYING LESSONS ON GROUNDS OF INSTINCT, BUT THAT BROKEN WING REPAIR IS ESSENTIAL BEFORE INDEPENDENT AIRBORNE FLAPPING IS TO BE ATTEMPTED.

DEAR REM, IN ACCORDANCE WITH YOUR INSTRUCTIONS I HAVE BEEN STANDING IN THE PLACE WHERE I LIVE FOR QUITE SOME TIME NOW. MAY I PLEASE NOW BE PERMITTED TO MAKE MY WAY TO MY SETTEE? I'M FEELING RATHER TIRED.

Dear Dave Stewart from The Eurythmics,

Re: Who's That Girl?

Derek: You baffle me, sir. I have just heard your 'futurist smash' on Bournemouth's peerless Wave 105 Live and can most definitely assure you that there *is* most certainly more than 'just one thing I want to know'.

Dave Stewart from The Eurythmics: Derek, Annie was referring to the one thing she wanted to know at the time; she was upset and I don't think she wants to talk about it particularly now 30 years later!

D: My next door but one neighbour Gordon Gillard's nephew, Nathan, is a renowned polyglot who specialises in teaching foreign exchange students and has asseverated over a cup of organic Tick Tock and a Maryland Gooey cookie this morning that there is no such dialect as the language of love, as referred to in your above-mentioned recording, the closest parlances being Pashtu and Amharic as spoken by the indigenous peoples of Pakistan and Ethiopia respectively, which, he gleefully stated, sound a bit like 'Passion' and 'Amorous'.

DSFTE: This is where you need to educate Nathan and get his nose out of all those different language books and tune in to Oprah or read Dr Gary Chapman's best-selling book The 5 Love Languages. I'm not sure you should have asked Gordon's nephew who seems to be a bit of a Sveznalica (Polish for Know-All).

D: It cannot be escaped also that any vernacular, whether real or fictional, is extremely unlikely to slip from a lover's tongue given that the mastication enabling hydrostat is merely (not to be confused with the metallic wind instrument so dexterously handled by Mr Wonder in another of your hits) a mouth organ, and plays no part in the origin of any diaphragm-generated glossology, to say nothing of the fact that the spoken word is both impalpable and weightless and hence incapable of such a glissade.

DSFTE: Here, Derek, you completely misunderstand; this is the secret way the lovers were communicating, passing poetry on delicately printed transparent film whilst kissing (like those fish that tell your emotions by curling up). Annie caught them red handed and I was there. There is no use using Logic when love is at play, Derek.

D: Furthermore, and dismissing a person's breath after perhaps eating spicy food or sipping a chilled drink on the basis that said waft is most definitely a side-effect of and not the speech itself, it is not possible for any discourse imbued with temperature to emanate from a person. Even were such a feat to be achievable, I hope you will forgive me for observing that the scope in calefaction between ice cream and the sun offers up sufficient leeway to render the comparison redundant, on the basis that the optimum soft scoop dessert serving gelidity of 10 degrees fahrenheit contrasted against a solar surface torridity of 10 million degrees allows a more than generous ambit of 9,999,992 degrees (factoring in an extra 1 degree either side in deference to your descriptions 'cooler' and 'warmer').

DSFTE: I do see your point here but the said ice cream was being consumed sitting outside Marine Ices in Camden Town on a warm sunny day but still 92,960,000 miles from the sun so the transparent messages were simply warm on top and cool below.

D: Another moot or, if you will pardon the pun, 'mute' point concerns your analogy of dumb hearts being broken just like china cups. Firstly, the cardiac muscle, not being fitted with a larynx, cannot be thus silenced. Were you to be referring to the sound of its beat, this is created by the speedy and powerful closing of valves, the cessation of which would render the organ not aphasiac, but exanimate. Secondly, I am unable to equate a ruptured composite of bodily tissue with dropped porcelain crockery.

Finally, I think you may have me confused with someone else given that on account of my ongoing sciatica I can no longer sustain a pace much brisker than a gentle canter and am hence unable to run around with anyone at all, whether they be male or female.

DSFTE: So sorry to hear that, Derek. Not that you take everything literally but I must point out that leaving the left side of your brain behind occasionally can be liberating, like letting a dog off its lead in the park.

D: I have been told that you are a pop star of impeccable character and am confident, as asked in yet another of your successful singles, that you would not lie to me. Notwithstanding this admirable quality, clarification of the falsehoods as above outlined would be appreciated at your earliest convenience.

DSFTE: That's fine, Derek. If anything I've answered is still left unclear, then I'll ask Annie to clarify further.

Yours,

David A. Stewart
Weapons Of Mass Entertainment

Dear Cher,
In your 'anthemic ballad' If I Could Turn Back Time, you indicate that were you to have the ability to travel to the past you would put it to use not by perhaps preventing the birth of Adolf Hitler or changing the course of the Titanic, but instead through not irking a previous partner. This, like the employment of a Hoover attachment in another of your hit records to achieve a jarring 'vocal effect' rather than using it to clean your house, is yet another example of abusing technology for your own ends!

Dear 'T.V. Smith' from The Adverts,

Re: Gary Gilmore's Eyes

Although initially sympathetic to your dreadful quagmire that was the keratoplasty leading to the gift of sight by way of an executed scofflaw, I regret that even the most perfunctory research into the events surrounding the expiry of said malefactor and his subsequent corneal donation contrasts with your version to such a degree that you may have either suffered the discombobulation sometimes associated with an administration of a local anaesthetic intrinsic to the operation, or may be accused of peddling, if you will pardon the pun, a 'tissue' of lies.

Assuming for a moment and for the sake of conjecture that you are speaking the truth, I can only despair at the ignominious unprofessionalism exhibited by the physicians engaged in the condemned felon-bestowed visual perception surgery itself, and also the abysmal peripheral medical personnel aftercare service. As even the most benighted viewer of Holby City will attest, The Hippocratic Oath would forbid the divulgence of any personal information pertaining to the original, in this case lawbreaking, ocular nerve user, to the donee, under any circumstances.

This serious ethical breach is further compounded by:

a) the unconscionable demeanour of the practice nurse on duty, whose abecedarian medical training relating to bedside manner, which demands an unstinting retention of composure and the suppression of all displays of emotion which may elicit convalescent malaise in what is already a highly stressful milieu, leaves much to be desired,

   and

b) the aloof practitioners who seem to be arbitrarily circumventing your bed.

If, as I suspect, there have been other historical concerns raised against such malpractices as a 'sister' looking anxious and quivering in fright and doctors who are complicit in avoiding their recuperating charges, then I would be highly alarmed if such a litany of derelictions had not been already promulgated to the Patient Advice and Liaison Service, resulting in a suspension of all ophthalmology at the hospital pending thorough investigations by the Care Quality Commission. That the reaction of the staff is probably denotative of a dispatched transgressor sensory organ transfer's unknown perniciousness (which should have abrogated the procedure in its preliminary stages on moral grounds) only fortifies the pressing need to truncate the department's ineptitude.

In relation to the transplant itself I regret being unable to afford you the luxury of postulative indulgences, on account of its methodology consolidated by the concise chronicling of the case in question.

Contrary to your chorus, the light-reflecting cornea, accounting for roughly 66% of the eye's entire optical strength, is the only element vital to an implantation given that it is fused onto the heir's pre-existing ball. Although you are correct in stating that the defunct convict furnished his observation apparatus to a third party, the post-fatality bequeathment was not to ameliorate anatomical erudition for the benefit of mankind as you claim, but to help two people who were presumably squinting a lot. To deduce that you are one of them specifically because you have heard on the evening news that a 'murderer's been killed and donates his sight to science [sic]', is analogous to watching The National Lottery Live and surmising that you have won without checking your ticket, simply because the draw has taken place. In addition, it is clearly documented that both ocular segments were adhered into their new beneficiaries a few hours after being enucleated from the recidivist's cadaver following his Utah-hosted morning demise. The flight duration from Salt Lake City International to Heathrow of 11 hours, allied to the peeling off of bandages (suggesting that the aciurgy had been performed some considerable time prior) just antecedent to the topical bulletin, unfortunately leads one to ratiocinate that your reasoning is indeed illogical on all grounds.

Even if the above-outlined perpetrator liquidation aftermath chronology had been linear, Mr Smith, and it could be verified beyond doubt that you were his 50% viewing ability inheritor, you would at best be looking through *part* of *one* of Gary Gilmore's eyes.

Forgive me also for pointing out my concerns relating to your supposed amelioration. Firstly, when Noel Edmonds introduced The Adverts on, ironically, a non-commercial television channel recently, you were clearly wearing thick-set spectacles of an excessively dark tint, strongly suggesting that without them you would have been wincing in the Top Of The Pops 2 studio light. Also, I can only posit that there must have been a great many complications affiliated to the grafting, which is usually undertaken simply by numbing the sphere in its socket, administering a sedative to its owner, affixing the iris coating and sending them home. Both the enforced hospitalisation and above neck mummification that you recount are normally completely unnecessary, unless of course the infirmary is engaged in unorthodox applications which, culpable with the afore-referenced complacency of its infrastructure, are sufficiently negligent to explain why your vision has only slightly improved, if at all. If you have not already considered the 'laser route' or simply wish to consider a stronger prescription, I would be happy to recommend Adrian at Dexter's Opticians in Southbourne Grove.

The entire foundation of your song is built upon on a skewed polemic, Mr Smith, namely that the incorporation of a wrong-doer's body part(s) into one's own could somehow besmirch the recipient with their personality, characteristics and/or memories. Arguably, in the case of cerebral matter, there may well be a metaphysical case to answer, albeit a contentious one. However, all other anatomical corporeality, not being sentient, cannot exert such influence. Eyes are simply lenses converting received light into data transmitted to the brain, nothing more. It is therefore as safe to look through Gary Gilmore's eyes as it is to use garden shears with his hands or remain compassionate with his heart.

Finally, I hope you will forgive my clichéd supposition that, being a 'punk rocker', your social ideologies would be at variance with undergoing privately funded treatment. Assuming this to be the case, the antithetical acts of you smashing a light in anger and pushing 'your' bed against the wall delineate an ignominious paradox. I too am from a working class background and thus wholeheartedly ratify the proletariat benignancy underpinning the constitutional foundation of the NHS. Therefore, with resources already stretched to breaking point, this ward entrance berth barricade and profligate bulb decimation (to say nothing of the reference to the frame actually belonging to you when in fact it is the property of the state, funded by your fellow basic rate taxpayers) could be construed as a disconcerting exposé of your egalitarian duplicity.

Yours,

Derek Philpott

PS My wife Jean has light-heartedly asked if you are in any way related to Telly Savalas?

....

Dear Mr Philpott,

Don't think for a moment that I don't appreciate your exhaustive, if not obsessive, analysis of Gary Gilmore's Eyes.

You have, however, rather misunderstood the concept of songwriting by comparing it with factual reportage.

Despite your concerns, I have never been under the impression that I was the recipient of the aforementioned peepers. For the avoidance of doubt, Gilmore was shot on 17th January 1977 and I didn't even

visit a hospital on that date. I have just checked my old diaries to make sure. I did have a dentist's appointment but I think it's highly unlikely they could have slipped in a corneal graft along with the small amalgam filling on my right incisor without me noticing.

No, the lyrics were just a bit of good old fashioned fun, pure speculation of the 'what if...' kind. Lighten up a bit, my dear chap.

With best wishes,

TV

PS You could learn a lot from your lovely wife Jean's attitude. I was most amused by her comment. Has she perhaps considered a career on the stage? The comedy circuit is crying out for some real talent.

DEAR THE STRANGLERS,
AS IS PATENTLY APPARENT FROM MANY
PHOTOGRAPHS ONLINE, MINE IS A HAIRSTYLE
TRADITIONALLY REFERRED TO AS A 'SHORT
BACK AND SIDES', AND YOUR STRAND
ELONGATING PSEUDO-THREAT IS UNLIKELY
TO APPLY TO ME PERSONALLY. JEAN, HOWEVER,
IS NOT AVERSE TO THE ODD PERM AND
ASSURES ME THAT UNSAVOURY ANECDOTES ARE
NOT SUFFICIENT IN THEMSELVES TO MAKE
HER CURLS STRAIGHTEN OUT, STRAIGHTEN
OUT. SHE THEREFORE RECOMMENDS THAT SAID
DISTASTEFUL RECOUNTINGS CAN ONLY ACHIEVE
YOUR CONCLUSION WHEN AIDED BY HOT TONGS
AND SOME SORT OF SERUM OR EQUIVALENT
PRODUCT, SUCH AS JOHN FRIEDA'S FRIZZ
EASE.

Dear Kajagoogoo,

I was sorry to learn from your '80s favourite' that your muse appears to be suffering both from ankyloglossia and respiratory problems. The former affliction, which, as you are no doubt aware, is a congenital anomaly restricting mobility of the tongue, may well, when attempted to be pronounced, cause 'oh' to be 'ah'.

You are to be congratulated, Kajagoogoo, for providing the pop charts of 1983 with this ingenious illustrative example of the ailment's symptoms.

However, although advances in biological science do 'move a little closer' to greater breakthroughs at an impressive rate, your implication that being tongue-tied and short of breath is also causal of acute bashfulness is one which I am sure would be open to question on the NHS Choices website. Furthermore, in the absence of source material, one feels it somewhat unfair to report, especially as unqualified pop stars, that modern medicine falls short of her complaint, considering that, for example, Benzodiazepines and selective serotonin reuptake inhibitors have a proven track record in combating anxiety disorders.

Finally, if you will excuse my slight facetiousness, it is hardly surprising that the poor girl is displaying signs of apprehension if she is being instructed to not even try and then try a little harder within a period of a mere two seconds.

Now Hush Hush yourselves and give the girl some space!

Yours,

Derek Philpott

PS I was going to say 'Hang On Now' as regards your assertion that dilation may be achieved whilst moving in circles, but you are in fact quite right. My wife Jean and I were recently sat 'in the round' with

friends at an 'all-you-can-eat' Chinese restaurant, and *did* find ourselves expanding after probably two too many trips to the buffet!

....

Dear Mr Philpott,

Many thanks for your concern regarding Joyce.

You may be glad to know she has now returned to full health and is
enjoying life at a more sedentary pace.

However, I must point out that her condition was not, as you
assumed, brought on as a consequence of repetitive mispronunciation strain, but moreover from attempting to get her larynx around
my big apple. In this particular case, the one which had procured me
first prize in the Beds and Bucks County Fair.

You see, I pride myself on my fruit growing skills, and Joyce has
enjoyed my plums many times before contracting Gastroesophageal
Reflux Disorder.

I trust this will put your mind at rest.

Kindest regards,

Mr Nicholas Beggs

Dear Mr. Hawkes,

Our neighbours Wilf and Olive enjoy your pop classic, I Am The One
And Only so much that they decided to send a message on 'Facebook'
to express their admiration via your 'other folder'. However, there
appear to be 68 of you. They are now a bit confused.

Whilst writing, I hope you will not mind my disclosing that I could
not help but observe an egregious inconsistency between a 'central

lyric' and the promotional video accompanying your 'inspirational teen anthem', which requires effusive elucidation. You state that you 'can't wear this uniform without some compromise' because I will find out that 'we come in different shapes and sizes'.

I am nonplussed, Mr Hawkes, and we have been thus far unable to determine from 'Google Images' any armed forces unit, paramilitary organisation, security firm, emergency service, educational facility, or fast food outlet whose personnel, students or employees are non-variantly and identically identifiable by denim jeans and an open-necked shirt, patterned in a style not unredolent of the duvet cover in our spare room. Or, indeed, how such unconventional and informal or 'casual' regalia could be in any way non-concessionary, purely on the basis of varying human contours and scale.

On a lighter theme, I am pleased to note that we have something in common, in that we have both 'been a player in the crowd scene'. Mine was when I was briefly witnessed as an uncredited extra in Softly, Softly, circa 1968. I am keen to secure a VHS cassette of this episode to show to our Tuesday night Gala Bingo partners who, sadly, do not believe me.

I appreciate your invitation to call you by your name, call you by your number to both compliment you upon your 'sound' and discuss the issues above-mentioned, however feel that such an approach could be construed as conducive to unjustifiable overfamiliarity, besides which no landline or cellular specifics are noted on any of your many numerous 'profiles'.

I therefore look forward to a more conventional, textual response at your earliest convenience

Yours,

Derek Philpott (and Wilf Turnbull)

Dear Derek and Wilf,

Thank you kindly for your very in-depth and insightful letter.

As you more than likely know, you probably should have addressed this particular correspondence to the very talented and surreal lyrical bard, Nik Kershaw, as the song in question was penned by him. Him and him alone. You could say that he was the one and only person involved with the writing of said song. (Not that, having read a lot of your writings, you would be as obvious with your literary puns.)

That said–

Your reference to 'coming in different shapes and sizes' touched a nerve with me. You may or may not know that for some years I have been working under the radar with a number of like-minded folk to counteract the damaging effects of the movement against obesity that now dominates this country's thinking. I have therefore gone out to libraries, bingo halls on occasion, and also at times delivering my message from a soap box with the aid of a portable public address system (PA in the modern jargon), most recently in Whitehaven in the north west of the country where I was warmly cheered by a small but appreciative audience made up of four sheep farmers, their dogs and six rugby players.

My campaign is titled… you've guessed it… we come in different shapes and sizes… and my mission will not have been completed until there is universal acknowledgement that we are indeed entitled to 'come in whatever different shapes and sizes' we choose. It's perhaps early days but, who knows, there might be a 'different shapes and sizes' political party one day. No? You don't think so?

Yours with High Hopes,

Chesney

Dear Roxy Music,
I am rather affronted by your unqualified medical advice. My friend Albert had his appendix out last Thursday and, obviously experiencing acute discomfort as a result, was ordered by his clinician not to undergo any unnecessary strenuous activity for at least three weeks. Sadly his convalescence was somewhat marred by your recommendation that he dance away the pain, concluding in ruptured stitches, a spoilt dressing gown, stained rug and an awkward return to hospital. Your foppish frontman is, in my opinion, a charlatan, whose guidance should be avoided at all costs.

Dear The Carpenters,
I fear you have been misinformed. From personal experience my tendency to throw them breadcrumbs is the primary reason why birds suddenly appear every time I am near!

Dear Ralph McTell,
I am surprised that I have to bring this to your attention, sir, but yesterday's paper would actually be 'telling' news of the day before yesterday!

Dear Mr. Wilson,

Re: Mary's Prayer

If there is one thing that my wife Jean cannot abide, Mr Wilson, it is what she colloquially and charmingly refers to as a 'waste of electric'. Our last tumble dryer was only most previously permitted to be utilised when suddenly the rain came down contrary to Ian McCaskill advocating a full drum. 'Standby' is frowned upon, and all rooms must be re-darkened upon exit, even if I have every intention of going straight back in.

She was therefore particularly piqued, and not to say a little befuddled, to hear your empyrean firmament energy wastage adjurement on Dave Bradford's Request Show as we made our way to The Salad Centre for brunch yesterday.

To the best of our knowledge, Daniel, celestial effulgence is generated by divinity, and we can locate no reference on the excellent Bible Gateway 'website' to said sacred luminescence being connected to a filament and power station or back up generator in the hereafter for the well-behaved. Although soaring energy costs applying in a transcendental catchment area where 'everything is wonderful and everything is free' are admittedly doubtful, we still consider your implication that hallowed salvation may be attained by those that 'leave a light on in heaven' positions your claim that you *used* to be so careless squarely in the present tense and sets a rather poor example to the earthbound, many of whom are at the mercy of EDF or on a Pay-As-You-Go key meter.

On an unrelated matter, with regard to your healthy food dislodging tip, I fear that you may be misleading your 'sophisti-pop following' somewhat. At our old house we were lucky enough to have a very sturdy tree in the back garden that blessed us with many a strudel. In my experience 'if you want the fruit to fall' you do not 'have to give the tree a shake'. Any attempt to vigorously jiggle a steadfast and mature trunk will only result in a resolutely static stem and a possible hernia in the case of the hapless bole shudderer. 'The bough is going to break', Daniel, under no circumstance consequential to an ineffectual disturbance to a stalk of some girth way beneath the targeted limb. As for your assertion that Mary can blow you up there if you cannot reach the top of the tree, Jean sometimes has a dizzy spell just from trying to cool her soup down, hence I fail to fathom how any lady of like stature can summon sufficient breath to hoist a full grown man to an utmost vertical foliage point of up to 12 metres.

In conclusion, therefore, if you are ever afforded the opportunity to re-inform your listeners of the least hazardous method of picking apples, pears, or cherries, it should be to pluck them off from a step ladder securely held by a third party.

I trust that the above observations have been informative and look forward to any further deity-petitioning balladry being of an accurately 'green' nature overall.

Yours,

Derek Philpott

....

Dear Mr Philpott,

Thank you for your concerned epistle. I'll try to address your points thoroughly as they are all worthy of examination and, I hope, some explanation.

To address your first issue, it would appear that you have misheard or misinterpreted the final line of the chorus as 'leave a light on in heaven'. This is quite understandable as you were listening on a (perhaps not perfectly tuned) radio in a noisy motor vehicle. However, the line is actually referring to the fabulous and, I'm sure you and Mrs Philpott will agree, sensuous saxophone of the musical artist Le Valedon who quite literally transports me to heaven with the tender toot of his horn. Unfortunately in the recorded version of the song, I mistakenly pronounced his name 'Lee Valeidon' as the typeface on the album sleeve for his lovely 'Sensuous Sax: The Night' is unfathomably small and my eye-glasses were in at Gregory Pecks the Opticians being repaired after I had damaged them during a game of Scrabble (don't ask!). I do apologise for any confusion caused by my amaurotic mispronunciation.

On your second point: This line of lyric has actually been a point of great consternation to me ever since that harrowing mixing session back in the late summer of '86 when our wily record producer David

Bascombe made the discovery that for every second he cut from a song his mixing time was reduced by around twenty minutes. By reducing the length of the song by four seconds that day, he was able to get home for dinner a full hour earlier than planned, and believe me, Dave enjoys his dinner. Unfortunately while he was callously slashing out four seconds of musical magnetic tape with his omnipresent editing razor he also removed a number of vital words from the lyric. I'm sure you'll agree that my original line 'If you want the fruit to fall into your wicker basket before winter takes hold you have to give the tree a shake using the correct gardening tools and wearing the proper protective clothing' was far superior in every way. Of course none of this was of any concern to Mr Bascombe, who went on to great success producing Tears for Fears' seminal Sowing The Seeds of Love (which in its original demo version was four weeks long).

If I may refer you at this point to Alphonse Du Breuil's The Science and Practice of Grafting, Pruning and Training Fruit Trees: Primary Source Edition, you will see that without human intervention, come winter most fruit trees will shed their fruit involuntarily and that man has over the centuries devised countless ingenious ways to beat Mother Nature to the harvest, as it were. Although Monseiur Du Breuil is keen to point out that it's not the most ideal of techniques, on pages 2135–2139, he goes in some detail into the various methods of 'shaking', 'worrying' or 'harrowing' the fruit from the trees. A small aside, but one worth making, I believe.

Finally, I think issues three and four can be addressed together. You see, at this bridge point in the lyric I am actually referring to Hurricane Mary and not the same Mary whose departure I lament in the body of the song. Hurricane Mary hit the coast of Florida in August of 1965 unleashing untold damage on persons and property and causing many a bough to break and no doubt much shaking of trees and harrowing of fruit, but thankfully, no deaths.

I hope that this has cleared up at least some of your concerns and that you and Mrs Philpott will in future be able to enjoy the song when it comes on the radio comforted by your deeper understanding and hopefully appreciation of the lyric.

Warm Regards

Daniel GC Wilson

....

Hi Derek,

Thanks for the huge laughs, absolutely wonderful letters! Though you might be interested in my reply to Gary…

> Somewhat entertaining; however, I should like to point out that, using your arithmetic, by the judicious cutting of 4 seconds of music, I would have been able to get home for my dinner one hour and twenty minutes earlier, not just the one hour you state.

> However, apart from this slight discrepancy, I lolled.

Yours,

Mr Bascombe (producer)

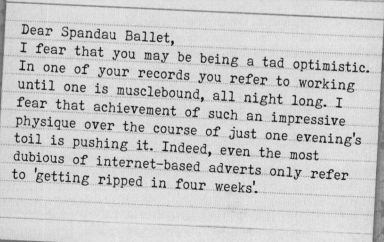

Dear Spandau Ballet,
I fear that you may be being a tad optimistic. In one of your records you refer to working until one is musclebound, all night long. I fear that achievement of such an impressive physique over the course of just one evening's toil is pushing it. Indeed, even the most dubious of internet-based adverts only refer to 'getting ripped in four weeks'.

Dear Tears For Fears,

Re: Sowing The Seeds of Love

Just a couple of things, Tears For Fears, and sorry for the rushed nature of this letter but I'm just in Argos at the minute. Our cat Gladys fetched up her Gourmet Gold Ocean Treat over my recliner earlier and I am waiting for my number to come up for a squeaky clean big chair.

1) Despite your assertion that the Love Train rides from coast to coast, please forgive my countering that The O'Jays' transportation venture may be doomed to failure. People all over the world joining hands, apart from being a logistical nightmare would, if achievable, which is highly dubious, start a love CHAIN, on the basis that a ring of individuals loosely connected at the wrists could in no way be construed as a Homo sapiens locomotive.

2) I find the concept that the DJ's the man you love the most to be quite offensive; to hold someone that merely plays records through an amplified system in higher esteem than male blood relatives, most specifically one's father, who is surely more qualified to such an accolade unless on Jeremy Kyle to undertake an 'all important DNA test', is just not on, sirs.

3) Re 'Food Goes To Waste', how this embarrassing topple has come to your attention is open to debate, but I confess that I *did* slip on a discarded McMuffin in the Botanical Gardens earlier this week which *did* result in egg on my face and mud on my shoes and I do intend to contact Claims Direct with regard to this matter as soon as I have finished my Christmas shopping.

Right, 603 it is, sorry, hope to hear from you soon.

Bye for now!

Derek

Dear Derek,

Thank you for your letter and your suggested corrections.

Firstly, the Love Train was a real and not a metaphoric train. It used to run non-stop from Los Angeles to New York; going west it was the Amtrack #378 and going east #379. It got its name from the amount of sexual activity that went on during the journey, and the noise amounting from such activity made it very unpopular with railway guards. This led to the great railway guard strike of 1973 (you may well recall that). As for your remarks about the O'Jays, I think you need to direct them to the band itself, though I think you've failed to miss the point about hygiene. I believe that in those days, we didn't have the hand sanitisers so omnipresent in hospitals and offices presently. People all over the world joining hands could lead to a calamitous spread of nail fungal disease. I've had it, my wife's had it, and I wouldn't wish it on anyone.

As for your point 2. I agree, the DJ cannot be held in higher esteem, unless of course that DJ happens to be Doctor Janov. His work has influenced us greatly. I don't want to labour the point here but it may come in handy if you read Primal Man (A New Consciousness.) I can send you a copy if you give me your address.

Point 3, I'm very sorry to hear about your mishap and wish you well with Claims Direct. The original line was 'Food goes in the waste disposal,' but it just didn't sound quite right.

Good luck with the Christmas shopping.

Roland Orzabal on behalf of Tears For Fears

Dear Vic Godard,

I am afraid, Vic Godard, that I am rather bemused at the concept of an electrified subterranean track splinter group. One wonders if your 'backing band', Subway Sect, are in actuality a radical faction of trainspotters perhaps exaggerating the volume of observed rolling stock ticked off in their notebooks for financial gain in order to use this deceit as a 'platform' to fulfill an immoral 'Ambition' to 'Split Up the Money'.

That the rogue locomotive observation data-distorting cult were often to be presented sporting cardigans in your 'early promo shots' does little to detract from this hypothesis. Indeed, it could be argued that their brazen public displays of knitted-sweater wearing surely only serves to emphasise that 'nobody is sorry', or indeed scared, in relation to any repercussions owing to said below ground chicanery.

In the presence of such a malevolent rail clan, and no matter how drowsy, you may be assured that I will from now on do my utmost never to lose consciousness on any buried cosmopolitan network, or indeed, heeding the extremely sensible advice of Petula Clark, sleep in the Subway even at ground level. After a brisk stroll on the front some months ago I repaired to their branch on Commercial Road for a Meatball Marinara foot-long 'on' Hearty Italian and dozed off at my table for a few seconds. Imagine my outrage, therefore, to be awoken by a posse of errant schoolchildren blowing Sprite at my spectacles with straws and attempting to insert the tightly screwed-up corners of serviettes into my ears whilst saying 'Let's make him Dumbo.'

Whilst writing, I must take considerable issue with your outlandish claim that everyone is a prostitute singing the song in prison. Were the entire population of the world to be custodially serenading 'ladies and gentlemen of the night', Vic Godard, the following insurmountable incongruities would apply:

1) the target market of potential clients to solicit to would be non-existent;

2) even were the above point not to apply, the incarceration of said remunerated courtesans (for 'twenty odd years' or fewer) would nullify their ability to canvass upon traditional pitches such as but not exclusive to the following:
   • Street corners
   • Red light areas (not to be confused with heaters found in the outside smoking areas of pubs and clubs)
   • Amusement arcades
   thus ceasing trade;

3) were both of the above problems to be resolved, the monopoly of contracted concubines flourishing to the extent of excluding all other occupations would naturally ensure that there would be no prison officers, convicting magistrates, people to build said facilities or, for that matter, chefs, plumbers, cleaners or any organised society whatsoever.

Oh, well. Tata for now!

Yours sincerely,

Derek Philpott

PS The wall is not a bad religion, sir. It is a non-denominatory partition between two areas.

....

Dear Mr Philpott,

Thank you for your letter. I do hope I can dispel at least some of your bemusement.

On the other hand, I may just deepen it.

Firstly I will admit that as a youngster I made regular forays to Kings Cross Station, half-pencil behind ear and Ian Allen in blazer pocket; however, the notion of seeking or expecting to make financial gain from the fruits of any such activities is frankly a harebrained suggestion. Furthermore, our inspirational underground passage is of the pedestrian variety, namely the dank, poorly lit Hammersmith Broadway underpass, and I can only say I am cut to the quick by your mockery of our image crisis.

I am relieved that you won't be sleeping in any subway entrances anytime soon and strongly advise against further visits to the sandwich establishment you refer to. Should you find yourself peckish and in the Commercial Road vicinity, there are Prêts aplenty where I'm sure you and your spectacles will be treated with the utmost respect.

I admit that my claim that 'Everyone is a prostitute' is wholly dependent on how the listener or reader defines the word and therefore I can't fault the gist of your ensuing arguments. My only defence is that my words were the product of a teenage mind versed in virtual realities and that with experience and age has come the realisation that I should have considered the foundations before I started on the wall.

Yours respectfully,

Vic Godard

Dear Mr. Heaton,

I would like to congratulate you on your uncanny ability to predict certain events through your lyrics. Perhaps I should explain further.

A while ago, Olive's cousin Sylvia was distraught when her albino rabbit Thor escaped. A search of the garden proved fruitless, and Sylvia's thoughts were turning ominously towards the dangers of foxes and traffic. However, she then heard Old Red Eyes Is Back on the radio, and almost immediately Thor poked his furry albino head round her shrubs.

A short time later, our friend and neighbour Mike Molloy was encountering difficulties in his search for a practical, safe and reasonably-priced caravan. He then heard your 'a cappella' classic Caravan of Love and soon found exactly the right model at a bargain price. Mike is now the proud owner of a second-hand 'Sprite Finesse', and says that you would be welcome to join him and his wife Margaret in the New Forest at your convenience (although of course it would be impractical to invite 'every woman, every man', as it is only a four-berth).

Finally, Olive and I once scored a 'Perfect 10' in the notoriously tricky 'Popular Culture' round of the Sunday Night Quiz at the Commodore pub. What had been on the radio while we were getting ready? Perhaps you already know, Mr Heaton!

I think you would agree that there is more than mere coincidence at work here. I am put in mind of an old schoolmate who could 'smell' the future; I cannot recall his actual name, but he was known as 'Nostrildamus'.

On a more serious note, may I respectfully suggest that you concentrate on writing songs about desirable scenarios, in order to maximise your unusual talent to the benefit of others. For example, Olive and I would particularly like to hear a song which predicts the reintroduction of the delicious and much-missed 'Toffos', or one about a more frequent service on the 1B bus route, especially at weekends.

Of course, you are welcome to visit us at Turnbull Towers any time you are in the 'Beautiful Southbourne' area. If you call first I will check that we have an ample and varied supply of biscuits.

Best regards,

Wilf Turnbull

Dear Wilf,

For some time I've known I had this capacity to predict events, so it was with great excitement that I opened and read your letter.

You are of course correct that I cannily forecast personal happenings via the source of lyrical wizardry but I'm afraid you're mistaken in implying that I'm the only chart act to have done so.

The expensively trousered, yacht-hopping fops Duran Duran also had the ability to look into the lyrical crystal ball. Look no further than their massive hit Rio.

Just 18 years after the song charted, I met Rio Ferdinand on holiday in Malta and the lyrics 'I've seen you on the beach and I've seen you on TV' even shocked him when I sung them to him. He got so spooked out by it that his wife called the police on the 4th or 5th occasion I sang it to him and to be honest I don't blame her.

Another regular fortune teller was my old chart buddy Michael Jackson.

He foretold several things that happened to me, including Stranger in Moscow – when I went there accidentally after a few too many black cans which led to boarding the wrong train in Innsbruck, Billie Jean – obviously referring to my chance meeting with Bill Gates when I drunkenly mistook him for Billie Jean King and, perhaps most perniciously of all, his 1988 hit Dirty Diana, which for a variety of reasons I can't go into on these pages.

Anyway I wish you all the very best and hope you both continue to have fun long after your deaths.

All the best

Paul Hx

Is there life on Marsupials? **David Joey**

Here, boy! When you're with me. Here, boy! **Buddy Collie**

Mr Rick Hakeman

With or without oo-oo, ah-ah! **Bonobo**

The Love Carrots. **Rabbit Smith**

With the greatest of respect, **Miss Amy Winemouse**.

Happy talking, talking flappy talk! **Catfish Sensible**

Our latest Trilogy. **Elephant, Snake and Llama**

In a tree by a river. Our cover boy, **Mr Nik Krowshaw!**

Deer of the dark. **Moose Dickinson**

Feline baby. **Mick Jaguar**

Heaven knows I'm miserably slow. **Lorissey**

In the waterhole. **Fish**

Ready to sty… It's **Piggy Smalls**
(aka The Snoutorious P.I.G.)

Hell ain't a bad place to beef… It's Thundersteak!
Aberdeen Angus Young

Dear Mr Tull,
I was initially very impressed that you could bring me 'Songs From The Wood' (which would necessitate instrument amplification via a glade power supply) hence was disappointed to note that the recording was made at The Morgan Studio in Willesden. At best the work should be retitled 'Songs From Near St. Johns Wood'. I await this correction on future sleeves.

Dear The Divine Comedy,

In these times of something for nothing 'PPI Claims' and suchlike bogus offers, I was aggrieved to see you of all baritones jumping on the bandwagon on Absolute Radio this morning.

I fully concur, The Divine Comedy, with your observation that 'no' means 'yes'. I refused a seat on the 1C just last week (offered by a young man in a Halfords uniform) even though my sciatica was in full flow, on the basis that I did not want to be accurately perceived as a senior citizen. I think you will find, however, that although some sections of society, such as the elderly or those on certain benefits, are entitled to fee-waived sight tests and vouchers to help cover the cost of lenses and frames (which qualify as a discount and NOT a transaction devoid of charge), heavily subsidised borderline complimentary spectacles are usually refused to most other NI contributors. Don't be unkind, The Divine Comedy: 'Everybody Knows' this, and you are to be thanked for keeping your misleading gratuitous optical correction aid 'post-Britpop croonings' to yourselves in the future. Stating that glasses come free on the NHS is not only falsely raising the hopes of those whose earnings fall within the threshold of Personal Allowance for income tax purposes, but conceivably catalytic of bellicose abrasions at doctors' receptionist's booth counters nationwide and, specific to ourselves, Vision Express on Commercial Road.

On an extraneous matter pertinent to your advert about the coach, I am quite confident that if my sentience were compromised by multifarious variegated pitfalls I would personally draw up a list of all setbacks and do my utmost to prioritise and address each according to its existence impacting magnitude. Unless purchasing a one way ticket to a situation of improved circumstances, one's temporarily shirked misfortunes, from which a fleer can admittedly distance himself both metaphorically and unfiguratively, could very well be at risk of exacerbation. If, for example, an outstanding debt with a pay day loan provider has been referred to bailiffs who have visited the property in one's oblivious excursion-derived absence. Or, if in an instance of apprehension-fuelled absentmindedness, the gas has been left on.

Your suggestion therefore that I take the National Express when my life's in a mess because it will make me smile is both extremely irresponsible and no laughing, or indeed grinning, matter.

Furthermore, some years ago I went on a beano to Brighton in a work colleague-filled charabanc, and to lighten the mood on the return journey after perhaps a few too many tankards of Worthington E on the pier, I attempted to initiate a comradely rendition of Three Hundred Green Bottles, only to find myself the only employee in full voice, followed by being instructed by my erstwhile foreman Willy 'Won't He' Wallace to 'put a sock in it, Philpott' when only 11% along the wall. I was then temporarily ejected at Chichester Services. Therefore, contrary to your choral exhortation, you will hopefully excuse me countering that from personal enforced forecourt-alighting experience it is preferential that *nobody* sing whilst the single-decker is in motion (as also laid out under Section 8, paragraph 1 of the referenced operator's General Conditions of Carriage which clearly prohibits behaviour which causes discomfort, inconvenience, damage or injury to other persons).

I am also befuddled as to precisely how a feeble old dear, a screaming child, a student and a family man manhandling a pram could possibly be construed as 'all human life' (I have passed my concerns onto David Attenborough), and how, if the jolly hostess is the unfortunate bearer of a posterior of the principality-scaled proportions that you infer, she has managed to prise said nether quarters into a Scania K340 cabin measuring a mere 12.8 x 2.55 metres and not been previously brought to my attention through the medium of Channel 4's Bodyshock documentary series.

Notwithstanding the glaring disparities above-outlined, Jean and I, on the whole, 'love what you do', The Divine Comedy, and consider you to be the best turned out pop star we have encountered since the equally very clean Mr Clayderman, and vocally on a par with Tony Monopoly at his peak.

Well done!

Yours,

Derek Philpott

....

Dear Derek,

Thank you for your letter. I am sorry if some of our songs contain certain statements or analogies that you consider false or misleading. Please let me assure you that we take your comments very seriously, and that all customer feedback is immediately passed on to the relevant members of the Divine Comedy team for rigorous analysis. The systems our experts have designed for the creation, manufacture and delivery of our products are, we hope, of the very highest calibre. Divine Comedy composition specialists are drawn from all the great centres of learning across the globe, and are generously rewarded for their creativity and problem-solving abilities. Our state-of-the-art facilities in Hemel Hempstead have been designed to be the perfect environment for the production of unnecessarily orchestrated pseudo-intellectual post Brit-pop music, and have won many prestigious awards.

We recognise the high expectations you have of our products – expectations we struggle daily to fulfil. And we will continue to labour to reach, if not raise, the level of excellence for which we are rightly renowned throughout the world. It goes without saying that we value the needs of the consumer above all else. Therefore it is of the upmost concern when some of our recordings fail to attain the high standards that you, our highly valued customer, have come to enjoy over the years. Be assured we will endeavour to correct the textual inaccuracies that you have most diligently brought to our attention, and strive to prevent any recurrence of the fault. Please accept our most humble and sincere apologies. In acknowledgement of the trouble you've been put to, please find enclosed a £10 DC gift voucher*.

Yours sincerely,

Neil Hannon
Head of Customer Relations

* Voucher redeemable at any unnecessarily orchestrated pseudo-intellectual post Brit-pop music outlet. This free gift does not imply any guilt or wrong-doing on the part of the company. Must be used by 31/8/14.

Dear Messrs. Box,

Re: Your recent statement 'I'm a-Living In A Box'

We regret that we have been unable to ascertain your exact current whereabouts. However, while many habitable structures are indeed 'box-like', or cuboid, in shape, we feel that it is extremely unlikely that your place of residence can be described as a 'box' due to its primary building material (probably not 'cardboard') in addition to its dimensions and presumed contents.

Indeed, we were under the impression that 'pop stars' such as yourselves were awarded extremely generous salaries which would no doubt facilitate the purchase of luxury abodes. As you claim to 'know what's going on… in my mind', we suggest that a lexical misunderstanding, rather than a hallucination, has occurred.

Should, however, you have found yourselves financially inconvenienced, and are indeed living in an actual 'cardboard box', we are frankly surprised that you have made such a statement, as this unfortunate situation would appear fairly obvious. We trust that our time is not being wasted on this matter.

It is hoped that the above comments have been constructive, and look forward to the release of the 'follow-up' single, which we are sure will also reflect the style and glamour of the modern age.

Yours,

Wilf Turnbull and Derek Philpott (neighbour)

....

Dear Mr Turnbull,

On behalf of my fellow Boxians, I thank you for your correspondence.

We are quite excited to report that we all continue to reside in boxes of various sorts. None, I'm pleased to say, are constructed from Binder's board, card stock, corrugated fibreboard, display board, paper board, container board or any other sort of cardboard. We, sir, live in boxes which one could only describe as lavish beyond the imagination of the common man.

Living in Chiswick, West London, however, we were recently most concerned when the route for the Cross Rail Project was announced.

It appeared that it would threaten our well-insulated serenity and tunnel directly under our posh boxes! Taking pertinent advice from our own great song, Living In A Box, 'life goes in circles, around and around circulating, I sometimes wonder what's moving underground, I'm escaping...' we thought we might be in need of the services of a removals company and be on our way. Fortunately, this never became necessary as the planned Cross Rail tunnel route was changed at the last minute to go via Acton.

I remain faithfully yours,

Marcus Vere
Living In A Box

Dear Mr Gabriel,
We have some workmen outside resurfacing the road at the moment, and I very much doubt that upon completion of the task they are all expecting a free car simply for preparing the avenue that it is to utilise. Similarly, one suspects that those who tarmac runways are probably not anticipating a complimentary Boeing 737 at the end. Even disregarding the restrictions of my ongoing sciatica therefore, your stating that I could have a steam train if I just laid down my tracks is both utterly preposterous and misleading to any manual labourer whose hopes you may be unrealistically and — if you will pardon the pun — groundlessly raising. I BID YOU GOOD DAY, SIR!

You don't care where we go and you don't care what we do, you just want me to take you with me. Well actually, Prince, I was just off to Wickes to buy some curtain hooks. It's not going to be very exciting, I'm afraid.

Dear Culture Club,
Re: I'll Tumble 4 Ya. Thank you for offering to fall down with me in mind. However, I am at a loss to see how such an awkward descent could benefit me personally. If, however, you are somehow aware that our washer/dryer is on the blink and the dirty basket is mounting up a bit your offer is most welcome. Where shall we bring the bags?

Dear Toto Coelo,

Re: I Eat Cannibals

I regret to inform you, Coelo, that I am most disturbed by the lyrical content of your quasi-tribal musical offering. Despite the admittedly pleasant melody and rather hypnotic 'drum beat', I must object to your avowed pride in your macabre diet.

Moreover, cannibals are the diners of human flesh, rather than the dinees; they are by definition likely to eat you, and not vice versa. If, however, your claim is correct, I would like to point out that two wrongs certainly do not make a right!

Aside from my objections concerning the legality and ethics of your actions, I would take issue with comments such as 'Healthy recipe, what you got it's good for me' and 'Looks trim, vitamin, forget the dietin''. I am by no means a qualified doctor, but I have heard that human meat contains certain bacteria which are harmful, and feel that your claims to its nutritional benefits are frankly abhorrent.

Perhaps 'Ros Holness', a member of your savage cult I believe, recalls her father, Bob, hosting an unusual quiz on television in the 1980s. If Ros and her vile tribe are feeling peckish in future, I suggest they avail themselves of the delicious and morally neutral substance of honeycomb, which the Blockbusters board evokes so clearly.

I look forward to a considerable improvement in the quality of your lyrics, and eagerly anticipate your forthcoming release, Mucho Macho.

Yours,

Derek Philpott

....

Dear Sir,

Thank you for pointing out the dangers of our plight!!!

I was a vegetarian and suffered greatly with I Eat Cannibals. The fact that I succumbed to an illegal act which was celebrated all over the world had me awake for many a night (that and the rustling sound of the plastic bin bags we wore). Roastin' vitamins took me back to a vegetarian state of mind! But the power of 'eating cannibals' was so great that sadly I returned to being a carnivore, and life has never been the same since.

Anita Chellamah **(Toto Coelo)**

Dear Mansun,

In my younger days, far from clandestinely quaffing R White's, I was not unimpartial to stronger intake. My idea of fun, or should I say, that of me and the boys in the local football team, was to repair to the local bar after the match for a pint, even if the pre-game 'Everyone Must Win' pep talk had resulted in us being thrashed 14–0 by a squad of off-duty policemen.

One such excursion occurred on one of these days, after our central midfielder Tony Beasley had, like a fool, left a wide open space for an opposing Detective Constable to put the first of many past us with just a couple of little kicks, leading to our victory slipping away.

Obviously feeling negative, he so much wanted to make amends that he insisted on paying for all drinks for the whole side until the bar was closed for business.

I am sure that it comes as no surprise for you to learn of my fragile state and fall out of my bunk the next morning, replete with hopes that my then fiance Jean would forgive me for my disgusting state and not check under the bed, whereupon I foggily remembered having been quite ill.

Needless to say, I had imbibed more than I'd had before and more than I really needed. The special drink that knocked me for six, however, was a most peculiar concoction whereby one was required to lick some Saxa off of one's hand, quickly drink the clear contents of (from memory) an egg cup and then immediately chomp on a citric slice. It is imperative to relate that at this point of the evening we had been joined by one of the barmaids at the end of her shift, and that the slight grimace at the sharpness of the beverage's conclusive act was displayed by all, irrespective of gender, and not exclusive to masculinity.

Therefore, and notwithstanding the immaterial variant of biting into said fruit segment as opposed to the administration of a partial vacuum upon it, I am compelled to write this letter in the hope that you may soon be able to outline exactly how being a boy is like sucking on a lemon.

I also write with good intentions relating to your predicament of being situated within a vast expanse and gazing fixedly at thin air at the precise instant of a structural catastrophe. It is surely apparent from the very disclosure that the commodious area is shoddily canopied that you must be transfixed in a warehouse, aircraft hangar, shopping centre, pop concert arena or covered market. Although confused as to quite how a roof may crash in a daze, given that to the best of one's knowledge an architectural sheltering is incapable of experiencing bewilderment upon fragmentation, it is recommended that the insurers of said complex be contacted if you may have been harmed in any way as a result of said event, if indeed it can be proved to be resultant of inadequate workmanship.

Finally, as regards your alarming impartation that she makes your nose bleed, although I am somewhat befuddled at her ability to instigate your nasal haemorrhage, it is advised that you distance yourself from this unnamed female in social situations. If this is sadly not an option, make sure you've got a red hanky.

I have to go now chaps, as I'm expecting the electric man and he has not been here before so I keep looking out of the window in case he has got lost. I doubt that he will be 'bringing his sunshine to me' (no doubt inspired by Morecambe and Wise), however, but it's OK; I may well look at solar panelling at a later date but for the time being we are just having the meter changed to a different tariff.

Yours sincerely,

Derek Philpott

....

Dear Derek,

Thank you for your letter. I see you refer to many Mansun references in your correspondence; from R White's lemonade (from my long lost B-Side Lemonade Secret Drinker), to My Idea of Fun, a song about a psychopath – quite apt for the band Mansun. I'm impressed with your knowledge of the band's back catalogue, particularly the fact that Wide Open Space is a football reference, and not a tale of teenage alienation. Your knowledge of the band's songs is certainly far greater than most of the band themselves, and I'd be impressed to see how many Mansun fans spot the references to the songs in your letter. I'm not sure I know all of them myself!

I'm most impressed by you spotting that the lyrics from the chorus of Electric Man are indeed the theme tune from The Morecambe and Wise Show (I don't think I've actually made that public before, and it was quite a bone of contention in the band, I believe), but a girl once told me I was like a miserable version of David Bowie, and started sarcastically singing the theme tune from Morecambe and Wise at me, so I said I'd put together a song for her about it, and Electric Man was born; a cross between Morecambe and Wise and a miserable David Bowie. The odd thing is, you look more like a miserable version of David Bowie than I do these days, Derek…

Best,

Paul Draper

DEAR MARTIN FRY,
IF, AS YOU STATE, YOU FORGET EVERYTHING
WHEN SUCH AN EVENT OCCURS, IT IS STRONGLY
RECOMMENDED, ESPECIALLY WHILST DOING
A WEEKLY FOOD SHOP WITHOUT A LIST, OR
OPERATING HEAVY MACHINERY OR A MOTOR
VEHICLE, THAT YOU DO NOT LISTEN TO 'BEING
WITH YOU' OR 'THE TRACKS OF MY TEARS' ON
YOUR IPOD OR STEREO.

DEAR THE WURZELS,
MY UNDERSTANDING FROM THE LOCAL PAPER
IS THAT MUCH OF THE NATION'S FARMING
COMMUNITY IS BEMOANING ITS CURRENT
SUBSIDY-STRAPPED PLIGHT. YOUR PURCHASE
OF A BRAND NEW 'BLINGY THRESHER' IN
SAID CLIMATE AS OPPOSED TO A PERFECTLY
FUNCTIONAL SECOND-HAND MODEL, AND YOUR
GLEEFUL POP-CHART BOASTING, IS THEREFORE
'NOT ON'.

Dear Mr. Bragg,

Re: The Milkman of Human Kindness

Whilst it is most refreshing to happen upon such a benevolently magnanimous pop star willing and able to reciprocate to the general public in recognition of the money spent on concert tickets, records and merchandise, I fear that your delivery service has been, if you will pardon the pun, 'soured' by the nefarious activities of an unseen interloping nemesis.

Before I expand upon my suspicions, however, I hope you will indulge my elucidations germane to several perceived dissimilitudes within your sparse disclosure.

Much as I appreciate the sentiments of your offering to send poetry if I am poorly, I fail to grasp the pharmaceutical merits of the iambic pentameter. Admittedly, I was once briefly hospitalised after contracting food poisoning courtesy of an undercooked lamb dopiaza in a restaurant that I no longer patronise, and found my constitution strengthened considerably by the kind 1978 paperback gift of The Thoughts of a Late Night Knitter from a wellwisher. However, to posit that my speedy recovery was thanks not to intravenous saline rehydration and the excellent medical team and attention received at The Royal Bournemouth and Christchurch Hospital, but the holistic placebo that was the piquantly droll Pam Ayres stanza compendium is, at best, contentious.

You also state that you will wait whilst I am sleeping. If I am honest I find this intendedly munificent proposal to be more than just a little disquieting, to the extent that I very much doubt I would be able to even *achieve* a state of absent consciousness if aware of your potential abiding presence at some later juncture during slumber (especially due to the fact that I have recently viewed Paranormal Activity on Netflix and am reminded of a particularly harrowing scene). Indeed your further propoundment vis-à-vis you will dry my tears if my bed was wet could well be interconnected with the former on the basis that were I in fact to stir and witness you or any other protest singer unexpectedly looming over me in my own home, then nocturnal enuresis could well be a likely side-effect. In the case of such an involuntary but wholly understandable mattress moistening, I apologise but some fresh linen, a pocket Febreze and hairdryer set to high would be far preferable to the cheek and eye dabbing being proffered. Perhaps, all things considered, it would be better all round for you to pop home and then return around 9am, at which time I am usually up and dressed and ready for breakfast.

My wife Jean and I have taken to ordering our weekly shop via Ocado Online. This makes the whole business of selecting groceries a lot easier, as we can do so from the comfort of our living room and do not have to worry about traffic and parking. Unfortunately, a consequence of this 'lifestyle change' is that we no longer rely on Unigate to supply us with our regular four cartons of semi-skimmed, but simply add this to our internet 'basket', effectively rendering you redundant. It would also seem that you are delivering milk extracted from the altruism of Homo sapiens, and I am at a bit of a loss as to exactly how such decorum could be bottled.

For these reasons, and despite your introductory promotion, I am afraid we have chosen to remain with our current suppliers. Notwithstanding this impersonal rebuttal, it appears from your estuarial vocal that you have already frequented our doorstep and, having just checked outside my porch, I regret to advise you that it appears that the consignment has been pilfered, leading one to naturally conclude that you have a vindictive rival in the form of a Thief of Human Kindness.

I wish you luck in apprehending the bounder.

Yours,

Derek Philpott

Dear Mr Deckpot,

Thank you for your litter.

I fear you may have been the result of a misconception.

The offers made to you in my song The Milkman of Human Kindness are non-negotiable as stated in the terms and conditions of my poetic licence, section 5, clause VII, verses 4–9a.

They state clearly that I have been apprehended by the Milk of Human Kindness Marketing Board to deliver their gladsome product as and when is felt necessitacious and you, Mr Phillip Desktop, are on my round.

The process by which the Milk of Human Kindness is distilled and distributed is long and complex, involving patience, prognostication and precipitation.

As you will be aware, society is divided into two types of people: bad eggs, who are disgruntled with the world, and kinder eggs, whose overall outlook is positively gruntled.

The happiness that these kinder eggs generate rises into the atmosphere, forming clouds of jollity which, when they drift over vast deserts of despair, rain down as much needed chuckles, chortles, titters and tee-hees.

We catch these in a special receptacle that we call a 'dead pan'. As it fills, the dead pan breaks into a smile and releases the Milk of Human Kindness. We bottle this precious liquid and send it out into the woebegone of this world.

The Milk of Human Kindness has been shown to have great benefits to health and happiness, heartening the disheartened, upcasting the downcast and combobulating the discombobulated.

If you don't require the extra pint, Mr Crackpott, you are obligated to pass it on to someone in greater need than yourself. The Milk of Human Kindness cannot be stored and will curdle into lachrymousse if not immediately utilised.

I hope my response will leave you and your colleague Mr Turnip enlightened as to the nature of my task.

I remain,

Billy Bragg
The Milkman of Human Kindness

Dear The Human League,

My professional background is one of proofing and desktop reproduction. I have always been male and have never served drinks on licensed premises. Neither do I believe that we have ever been formally introduced.

Are you sure that you have the right person?

You have my assurance that were you to 'Dare' to select, vigorously convulse and then revolve me whilst in the discharge of clientèle aperitif distribution, I would have no hesitation in reporting you to the police force. I am quite confident, The Human League, that the Crown Prosecution Service would agree that my being picked out, shook up and turned around by an anthropoidal guild in the workplace would be in the public interest to pursue, and that, once steadfast, its mind could not be 'changed back', irrespective of presumed communal regret.

On a possibly related matter, given that such establishments are often popularly bedecked in such reflective surfaces, I keep feeling *agitation* at your heralding the imminent arrival of the mirror man, who is presumably on his way from the 'Warehouse' (not to be confused with the home of your previous keyboard player). It is not the speculum consignment per se which concerns, but his proclamation to be a 'people fan'. Assuming that the gentleman is not nonsensically referring to himself as a colony enthusiast, one finds it disturbing in this day and age that delivery drivers are so meagrely salaried that they feel compelled to take on second jobs manually ventilating socialising patrons to prevent them from 'Being Boiled' in poorly air-conditioned bistros.

I look forward to any spokesperson for your biped alliance 'Coming Back' when they have a few 'Seconds' to spare.

I remain yours sincerely,

Derek Philpott

PS My wife Jean has just pointed out that for many years she mistakenly thought you to be named 'Mangue' on the basis that she had never thought to pick up your 'Hysteria' album in record shops and look at the back. She now reasonably points out that matters could have been made much worse had you been called 'Humbug Lager'.

PPS Or 'Untold Fidgit'.

....

Dear Madam (or Sir),

Why, oh why oh why must I continually be taken to task concerning the ill-advised historical transgressions of my former colleague Mr P Oakley of Sheffield, S.Yorks?

As I have explained at length on countless occasions to the BBC, the CITV, the IRA, the NME and many's another well known institution and organisation; both yourself and all other would be 'plaintiffs' who irrationally feared being the recipient of one of Mr Oakley's deranged misdeeds by mistake of identity, can rest assured that you are definitely 'not the right person'! In point of fact, might I dare to

suggest that you are quite probably 'not right' at all.

At the time in question, some decades ago now, and I believe during the 'Thatcher Junta', Mr Oakley of Sheffield, S.Yorks was inflicted by an unfortunate medical condition which caused his hair to grow all down one side of his face, thus leaving him visually impaired. This condition was thankfully cured some years ago, but at that time, and whilst afflicted by this condition (medically termed 'Neuromanticitis'), Oakley unfortunately mistook several people or persons in the Sheffield, S.Yorks area for a cocktail waitress from Attercliffe, Sheffield, South Yorkshire by the name of 'Louise Oglesby'.

It should be blatantly obvious to all concerned that if indeed you were 'the right person', then by now you would have surely been 'turned into someone new', and can therefore no longer claim to be who you are at present!

I put it to you, Mr Pillpott, sir, that your accusations are both misinformed and unfounded, and that you are indeed talking out of ~~your arse~~ turn.

Re your 'related matter' concerning reflective surfaces; to mention the 'Mirror Man' in common parlance is akin to mentioning 'The Scottish Play' in theatrical circles. And you are right to feel agitated Mr. Phillspot, as you would certainly not welcome a manifestation of (*Da Duh Daaah…!*): 'The Reflective One'.

The late Michael Jackson spoke of 'starting' with him only scant years before his untimely demise – co-incidence, or who?

Depart and calculate mathematically!

For the time being

Yours, etc.

Major-General A.Humanleague rtd.(Mrs)

PS Unfortunately too many people also never thought to pick up said Long Playing Recording 'Hysteria', and many of those who did had mistaken it for the popular 'Def Leppard' Long Player of the same name. Coincidentally, The Def Leppard are also of Sheffield, South Yorkshire, England UK, and if you think about it, as they can neither spell the word 'Deaf' nor the word 'Leopard' correctly, then 'Mangue' might have been a suitable enough moniker for their own pop group?

PPS As per your stated vocation; I also do a spot of furniture restoration, and find that Ronseal products are ideal for obtaining that professional looking finish on reproduction 'antique' style desktops.

PPPS FYI: one can obtain a fine pint of 'Humbug Lager' at 'Bar Humbug', Brown St, Sheffield, S.Yorks, during the festive period.

Yours again and again and again and again and again and again, etc., etc. (six times).

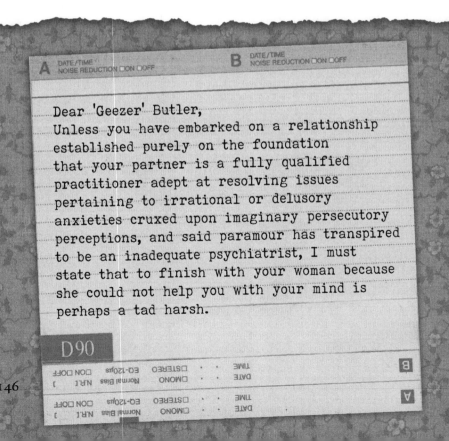

Dear 'Geezer' Butler,
Unless you have embarked on a relationship established purely on the foundation that your partner is a fully qualified practitioner adept at resolving issues pertaining to irrational or delusory anxieties cruxed upon imaginary persecutory perceptions, and said paramour has transpired to be an inadequate psychiatrist, I must state that to finish with your woman because she could not help you with your mind is perhaps a tad harsh.

Dear Toyah,

Re: I Want To Be Free

Although sorry to hear that you are bored, Toyah, I am also astonished. If my memory (which is admittedly not quite what it was) serves me correctly, then this is the first occasion on which I have had to write to a pop star pointing out that the very capacity that they are hankering after is not only already congenital to their present comportment, but jeopardised by the superfluous hijinks that they are desirous of executing.

To put it another way (or Toyah-tologically speaking!), you *are* free but your 'action plan' could well get you locked up.

Before I elucidate upon said heretofore maintained desiderium sabotage schism, however, I must bizarrely state that your reluctance to go to school and be somebody's fool could be both simultaneously and discordantly justified and unjustified for the following reasons.

Unless a tutor, invigilator, dinner lady, headmistress, substitute pedagogue, caretaker, other contractor or employee, or open evening invited parent or guardian, your class attendance at age attained 23 at the time of your UK number 8 'chart placing', a full seven years after pupils are required to cease lessons or GSCE testing, could be construed, in the parlance of today's youth (without reference to the aforementioned examinations), as an 'Epic Fail' and label you the dullard that you so yearn not to be dismissed as.

If, on the other hand, you were to be above categorised and are experiencing job dissatisfaction or fear of reproachment by proxy on account of your errant charge(s), then your disinclination is entirely understandable.

I do, conversely, wholeheartedly acquiesce in your rambunctious bellow exclaiming that you still have 'a brain up there' if you dye your hair, on the basis that my GP, Dr Trivedi, brusquely informed me when I called him in the middle of his afternoon session just now that the British Medical Journal has not recently featured any neurological/trichological fusion articles melding synthetic scalp filament tincturing to cerebral extraction, and could I please not phone him again during surgery hours, unless in the case of a genuine emergency.

In view of your current self-imposed quandary, I, with the assistance of my wife Jean (who has just returned from step aerobics and and is about to prepare drumsticks for dinner), have drafted, in order that you will hopefully remain incarceration free, 'The Wilcox Warranted or Wanton Wall Chart' or, if your current marital status is to be acknowledged, 'The Fripp Felonious or Fair Fact-Finder', an outline of which we present below for your consideration in an attempt to sustain your skewed whim whilst keeping you at large. This 'at a glance' guide, which, once honed, can be printed off immediately and sellotaped around your estate, will hopefully act as a handy and effective liberty preservation aid.

Here is the prototype for your approval:

Proposed Caper
'I'm going to turn this world inside out!'

Probable Outcome
Although bemused as to the machinations of such a magma-exposing globe crust reversal manoeuvre, the good news is that it is unlikely that you would be custodially punished. The downside, however, lies in the ineluctable certitude that this is wholly due to the legal system nominated to pass sentence, as part of all life on the planet, being expunged courtesy of your environmentally-unfriendly brouhaha. A further dyslogistic impact of your earth surface flip would be that your craving for that very element that by the virtue of your unique birth differentiates you from all else, i.e. 'to be you', would be nullified by your own self-inflicted expiry.

Proposed Caper
'Going to turn suburbia upside down!'

Probable Outcome
Again, whilst at a bit of a loss as to exactly how collective districts on the outskirts of cities or towns could be inverted at a gradient of 180 degrees, it is to be not unreasonably surmised that a successful multi-residential tract tilting could result in a lengthy 'stretch'.

Proposed Caper
'Going to crawl through the alleyways, being very loud!'

Probable Outcome
On the assumption that your sonorous walking on all fours buffoonery is not between narrow rows of houses that you own set within grounds boasting sufficient acreage to inhibit the hands and knees cacophony being carried to the ears of the local community, you may well find yourself subject to an 'Anti-Social Behaviour Order' (ASBO), which, if breached, could lead to tagging, and, if disruption to the peace of residents in built-up areas continues unabated, 'a spell in the clink'.

Proposed Caper
'Going to walk the streets, scream and shout!'

Probable Outcome
Substituting a horizontal meander with a vertical amble, this time in *front* of said premises (or retail outlets) as opposed to passageways to the rear, see previous probable outcome.

Proposed Caper
'Tear up the carpet and get rid of that!'

Probable Outcome
If you are proposing to uproot your own woven floor covering in your own property, so long as it is disposed of in a responsible manner, you should remain unfettered. Non-permission granted lower surface textile matting strippage within the dominion of another, however, such as, for example, a stranger's pied-a-terre or a DFS showroom, and/

or fly-tipping the dislodged tailored rug, could entail a stay 'At Her Majesty's Pleasure'.

Proposed Caper
'Tear down the wallpaper!'

Probable Outcome
Substituting dense fabric layering, a horizontal area and DFS with a decorative sheet, vertical area and a branch of Homebase, see previous probable outcome.

Proposed Caper
'Blow up the TV, blow up the car!'

Probable Outcome
The inflation of a novelty pool toy in the synthetically fashioned simulacrum of a vehicle or a television, or the digital enlargement of an image of said items utilising 'software programmes' such as Microsoft Paint are not autonomy imperilling. Actual entertainment system and saloon or hatchback detonation will equal 'pokey'.

Proposed Caper
'Sell all the magazines!'

Probable Outcome
Newsagent's shop proprietary is actually a lucrative and admirable endeavour, allowing, as it does, the ensuing profits from the sale of one's stock of current publications to be re-invested into the enterprise whilst concurrently enlightening and intellectually stimulating the general collective. If, however, you are contemplating periodical purloining, by way of the illicit removal of 'glossies' from, for example, a dentist's waiting room or a registered vendor, such as Cazip Food and Wine on Charminster Road, please anticipate 'bird'.

Proposed Caper
'Turf out the cat!'

Probable Outcome

Although domestic pet eviction is not penalisable per se, if it can be proved in a court of law, perhaps in the course of prosecution by the RSPCA under Sections 2 and 4 of the Animal Welfare Act 2006, that your feline abandonment knowingly exposed the hapless creature to predators, leading to injury or worse, in extreme circumstances you could reasonably expect to be 'taken down'.

Proposed Caper

'Pull down the abattoirs!'

Probable Outcome

Although arguably viewed as a principled deed in many quarters, slaughterhouse demolition, unless sanctioned by the carnivore appeasing profiteer(s) could find you 'in the slammer'.

Hopefully you will observe that, in the majority of instances, your celebratory shenanigans will ironically be consummated by that which you are exalting being removed. Given that you are obviously a very intelligent young lady, 'it's a mystery to me' that this jarring paradox has not previously been considered.

If it is any small consolation, internment would at the very least insulate you from the peak-based electrostatic discharges of your 'follow-up'.

We await your feedback.

Yours,

Derek Philpott (with help from Jean Philpott)

....

Dear Mr Philpott and your patient helper Jean Philpott (who I imagine looks somewhat like my old gym mistress Miss Boare),

I apologise for my ranting on the 1981 three minute diatribe called 'I WANT TO BE FREE', a rant against the educational regime I

had already left behind 6 years previously, but I just had to get my feelings of imprisonment and brainwashing out of my system. Also I wanted to attempt the first ever rap in the middle 8.

I wholeheartedly agree that, even though I have dyed my hair for 40 years, 'I still have a brain up there' and, as you kindly mention in your second to last paragraph ('Given that you are obviously a very intelligent young lady'), there are quite a few jarring paradoxes within this rambunctious adventure, but you have to take into consideration I hadn't eaten any chocolate for three days in an effort to look super-dooper thin for TOP OF THE POPS and I was as ratty as hell and dead cert on wreaking revenge on all those who thought I was an 'epic fail' at school.

I would like to point out in my defense, for all my failings at being a rebel I have opened the cages of many a small animal to escape to freedom, freed many a fish from those type of restaurants that have fish tanks, helped many an old lady across the road and sent many anonymous letters to journalists who write for the Daily Mail, let down many tyres on Porsche cars and have shouted out of my car window at those boys and girls who let their booty hang out.

Please forgive me and thank you for your very complex and wordy letter that took me three hours to read.

Toyah Willcox

PS 'I knew my Wife's lyrics were subtle, but had not fully appreciated their depth.' *Robert Fripp*

Dear The Manic Street Preachers,
I think I can help here as I used to have the same problem with my Lambretta which was always conking out. You either have a faulty fuel gauge or are ignoring it when it goes past red.

Dear Department S,

Re: Is Vic There?

'The night is young, the mood is mellow
And there's music in my ears
Say, is Vic there?
I hear ringing in the air
So I answer the phone
A voice comes over clear
Say, is Vic there?'

You will no doubt recognise the above as the pivotal and, indeed, only lyrics to your splendid 'new wave' telephone enquiry.

I am sorry, Department S, but 'Going Left Right' in the scanning of said text, I do not really know where to start.

Whilst the time of day and ambience outlined are not subject to debate, the fact that there is music in your ears is a clear indication that your call has been placed on hold or that you are in an automated queueing system. Therefore, if you will forgive me, to enquire as to Victor(ia)'s whereabouts of a taped recording is somewhat futile.

To then make no reference to replacing the receiver and yet hearing and responding to the ringing of an incoming call from a person *also* attempting to locate the self same person is most perplexing.

We really do need to clear this up, chaps, and in the meantime, considering that all in proximity to the device are clearly visible when an invitation is accepted, thus rendering similar enquiries unnecessary, I would recommend Skype as a far more economical and effective distance communication method.

Yours,

Derek Philpott

Derek.

It's the eternal quest for man's longing to find his inner self exasperated by the trauma of the modern techno industrial age… are we not all searching for our own Vic? But alas, the author of the fine but frugally penned words in the aforementioned song is no longer with us to add testimony to what might be their deeper inner meanings.

So it is to those of us left behind on this mortal planet to add interpretation to the lyrics or at least help impart some understanding to those that might be grasping this particular preverbal, lyrical and somewhat shitty stick from the wrong end.

As you point out, the ambience as well as the planetary alignments appear to be without question but after a moment's contemplation of this, or at least, upon watching one or two episodes of the most excellent TV programme The Sky at Night, you would soon realise that the relative positions of bodies in our solar system is forever changing. Consider it thus; we are moving through our solar system in an elliptical orbit around our nearest star (the Sun, not to be confused with your regular library reading of the daily newspaper with the same name) and our solar system is moving round the centre of our galaxy (the Milky Way, not to be confused with that deliciously tasting but albeit shrinking chocolate treat with the same name). The combined speed of around 483,000 miles per hour is breathtakingly rapid. Rather different to your meandering Sunday afternoon drives along the coast road from Bournemouth that you no doubt undertake with your dear wife Jean when the weather is clement. No wonder then there is ringing in the ears that could so easily be interpreted as 'Ringing in the Air'. I would think a one eighth of an anti clockwise turn on your hearing aid volume control would rectify this particular problem for you.

The perplexing issue of hearing a call whilst answering another can be readily explained through a rudimentary understanding of modern telephony systems such as using modern VoiP systems that can be configured to integrate with core applications like the CRM, ERP or ATS thus becoming an integral part of a business technology system. Things have moved on somewhat since the days of sharing a party line with which you may be familiar.

But this is all conjecture in the author's absence so sadly, we may never know the true meaning behind those frugal lyrics. It may well just as easy be that Vic was in fact just a nom de plume for Vaughn Toulouse himself and he may well have been talking to no one but himself in a particularly deranged moment. Either that or it may just be all made up Bollox.

Regards,

Department S

Dear Mr Harley,
I am assuming from your request that I come 'up' and see you that you are not on the ground floor. Sadly, as you make no reference to a lift and I am not good with stairs I would be more than happy to wait for you to make your way down, whereupon I may hand you the extra and spare Tommy Cooper joke book that I received for Christmas, which I am confident will elicit, at the very least, a wry grin.

Are you sure that you were 'born this way', Lady Gaga? May I say that I would be very surprised, young lady, if you *had* entered the world in a frock made of Kermit the Frogs with a telephone on your head.

Dear Technotronic,
I must politely decline your instruction to pump up
the jam. Not only do I fail to see how flavouring
can be enhanced by preservative inflation, but I
suspect that it may make a confounded mess of my
kitchen. Feel free, however, to contact me in the
future with any less unconventional cookery advice
that you wish to impart. Good day to you.

Dear Sad Café,

Re: Everyday Hurts

I potentially bring disturbing news, Sad Café, in relation to your perceived paramour, whose desertion has afflicted you with perpetual and alarmingly escalating discomfort. Judgement, however, with respect to the conjectural swain and your recent dereliction will be reserved pending the gleaning of further vital and profoundly pertinent data, as saliently detailed below:

1) Pertaining to the lamplight from her window, please clarify, if you are able, whether or not said fenestral luminescence was of a reddish hue.

2) You openly testify that you came up (indicating elevation to a higher floor) to her room to question her, and found her sitting all alone, contrary to your expectations. As no reference is made in your splendid vocalist's 'yearning delivery' to the means by which the premises were accessed, please specify if entry was achieved by way of a doorbell, knocker, communal buzzer, intercom system, debatable utilisation of the 'trades' button, or a partially or fully ajar street door. If the latter, as I grimly suspect, please verify if you

witnessed a sign in the hallway featuring a diagonal arrow pointed to an upper level adjacent to the word 'Model', perhaps hurriedly scrawled in heavy felt-tip marker pen.

3) With regard to the young man across the street who looks something like you and is walking with his head down to the ground that you espied when you looked down from the window, please furnish me with the following specifics. Was the imperfect doppelganger of a sheepish mien perhaps awkwardly pacing to and fro outside the tenement for some time as if summoning up the courage to cross the threshold? Were you of the impression that the youth was purposefully averting his gaze pavementwards in order to perhaps shield the exposure of distinct facial features from surveillance cameras situated on lampposts along the thoroughfare?

4) Would it be fair to state that there was a notable increment in police officers in the immediate vicinity of the apartment at around the time that your debatable inamorata had to go away?

5) Do you recall any of the vehicles in the surrounding locale travelling at a velocity far below the National Speed Limit and was any said transportation helmed by shifty and uncomfortable-looking personages?

6) Without prying too deeply into your intimate affairs, would you be able to confide if a telephone box had any role to play in your 'first date'?

7) Discounting any tokens or chattels which could be construed as standard fare within a burgeoning wooing, was there at any time an exchange of legal tender between yourself and your putative 'other half' and/or a guarded third party?

Upon collation of your feedback I will formulate my findings, but feel it only fair at this stage to warn you that they may not only be unpalatable but self-incriminatory.

On an unrelated note pertaining to your monicker, Sad Café, although it is perfectly understandable (although unacceptable) for the employees of a casual eatery to be sullen, perhaps owing to being forced to hand over all personal tips to the proprietor, disputes over shifts and/or overtime payments, rude customers or a combination thereof, said despondency cannot be extended to the bricks and mortar itself. That said, my wife Jean and I agree this trading name to be pleasingly euphonic and, during an idle hour this evening whilst waiting for 'Allo, 'Allo to start on UK Gold, elected, with the help of our many 'Facebook friends', to compile a list of possible aliases evocative of it, which we understand to be customary in the event that you ever feel inclined to perform a 'secret gig':

- Unhappy Restaurant
- Upset Coffee Bar
- Distressed Greasy Spoon
- Lacrimose Deli
- Melancholy Bistro
- Morose Carvery
- Pee'd Off Pizzeria
- Downhearted Buttery
- Dejected Snack Bar
- Teary Tea Shop
- Woebegone Grill
- Whingy Wine Bar
- Despondent Diner
- Mournful Luncheonette
- Disconsolate Truckstop
- Inconsolable Brasserie
- Regretful Refectory
- None Too Chuffed Chiringuito
- Heartbroken Hot Dog Stand

We look forward to hearing from you shortly, Sad Café, and hope that our light-hearted segue is of some comfort during this stressful time.

Yours,

Derek Philpott

Yo Wilf and Derek,

Thanks for the tome-like enquiry on our illustrious sojourn into 'ShowBIZz luvvy' via the wonderful classic Everyday Hurts (which, may I add, was originally designed as an ad for the car rental company Hertz).

I read with awe the quizzical first paragraph, and thought to myself: 'I hope he had a lot of gravy with that dictionary he's just swallowed!'

Whilst my reply might not be as lengthy as yours I will endeavour to answer all your probing questions and theories.

Let's get on then with

Point 1: The fenestral luminescence (oh gawd) was indeed red and there was a lit pumpkin carved with the legend 'No dwarfs' there too.

Point 2: Carrying on the link from Point 1, I can tell you that entry was made from the rear (careful now) which would explain the following lyric always being mistaken for 'Why did you have to go away' when in actual fact it's 'Why did you have to go OOH A'. Also 'more than I've been hurt before' would point to the room next door being reserved for clients with more of a dominatrix penchant.

Point 3: Not too difficult this one, as the street guy was actually her pimp touting for business, and keeping his head down for obvious reasons.

I think the above answer points would also emphasize the lilt in your remaining queries as to the nature of the establishment, and hope that it doesn't shock our loyal clientele after all these years. After all it was the biggest selling single of 1979 and was only pipped from the No 1 spot by that arse'ole Lena Martell's One Day At A Time (Sweet Jesus) which is to this day still our ultimate shame. This would explain the esoteric nature of the cogs and wheels (and backhanders) involved in the chart mechanisms of the day.

I cannot compete with your erudite and extremely comprehensive Egon Ronay list of your favourite cafés, so I won't!

But here's one for ya – Sad Café: where the tables are in tiers! (ARFF!)

One piece of research missing from your diatribe (kidding) is the origin of the band name.

It's from a well known US author called Carson McCuller's book The Ballad of Sad Café which apparently revolves around characters of blind men, circus dwarves, and prostitutes which leads us nicely back to Point 1 innit!

This has been a most enjoyable exercise, and may I suggest you carry it further if you wish by studying another of the band's greatest hits called 'MY OH MY' which contains lyrics right up your street.

Here's to our next meeting.

Fanx *Tara*
Sad Café

Dear Thompson Twins,

Re: Doctor Doctor

In response to your plea for assistance, may I point out that the fire services would be better equipped to deal with your predicament than your GP. I urge you to dial the emergency services on 999 immediately and ask to report a fire; I am sure, if your GP is as busy as Dr Greenwald at Southbourne Surgery, you will be pleasantly surprised at the firefighters' prompt attention.

Yours,

Wilf Turnbull

Dear Thompson Twins,

My apologies for my former correspondence, which I wrote in haste before listening to your statement in full. It is now my understanding that you attribute your dangerously high temperature to a deeply romantic emotion. From this information I now assume that you use the context as a metaphor to describe how you are feeling, and that you are not physically on fire. I wonder, however, if it is love you are feeling and not a touch of heart 'burn'. If this is the case a visit to your doctor may be appropriate, although I feel a pharmacist would be adequately equipped to advise you on the problem.

I thank you for your invitation to dance across the sea towards a destination you call 'Eternity'. As I'm sure we are all aware, to dance on water would be an impossibility. Therefore, I assume this dancing would take place on a secure vessel, an experience which would be most enjoyable. I gratefully accept. May I recommend Brittany Ferries' 'Barfleur' which sails from Poole, Dorset. If we were to take advantage of their midweek offer, the four of us could travel with a car for £29. This price includes the onboard entertainment which features a cinema, a bar area, and a disco, with live music provided by the popular duo 'Savoir Faire'. Unfortunately there is no discount available for family groups; in any case, the unusual numerical nature of your siblinghood (plus my own presence of course) may render our application for such a discount unsuccessful.

Please contact me again advising when you would like me to make our booking. The 'Barfleur' departs at 8am every weekday, and the crossing takes approximately 4 hours 15 minutes. The destination is Cherbourg in France, which is not 'Eternity' (I hope this doesn't disappoint) but a very nice town all the same.

Your friend,

Wilf Turnbull

Dear Wilf,

Thanks for your serial missives. Please forgive my lack of promptness in replying but I was unaware of your having made contact until very recently.

Firstly, to be absolutely clear: you have written to the Thompson Twins but it is I, Tom Bailey, who replies. I'm sure you understand that, for legal reasons, I cannot represent the views of all the group members.

Secondly, although I wrote the music and sang the song in question, I did not write the lyric. This was the work of Alannah Currie, to whom due credit must be given. Therefore, in your efforts to get to the bottom of this, my explanation must only be given the weight of a subjective interpretation, not a definitive author's opinion. But whilst I may lack the authority of the horse's mouth, I was at least in the same stable for a while – so here goes:

Yes, the song was about the fevers of wounded passion, but only on one level. I'm particularly fond of the triple-layered metaphor and, in this case, I decided one of its strata referred more generally to medical practice but also specifically to the NHS. You may be forgiven for thinking that was just my private way of getting through a tricky gig, but I can't miss the opportunity of drawing your attention to the way in which the once-noble organization has sadly floundered in the deep and murky waters of privatization since the piece was written. I remain hopeful that it will survive. So it's a sad song, but with a glimmer of optimism.

Which brings me to your generous offer of a group ticket on the ferry from Poole to Cherbourg. You certainly impress me with the thoroughness of some aspects of your research but, unfortunately, because I live in France, I would be travelling in the other direction. This rather puts us at cross-purposes so, regretfully, I must decline. However, now that we graze together on the lower slopes of Parnassus, I feel that I can get in touch if my schedule takes me within shouting distance of Poole.

Many thanks again for your message. I must confess, finally, that I was in two minds about my ability to reply. I think it was the picture of Bassett's Murray Mints on your website which pushed me over the edge: it should have been a Nuttall's Mintoe.

Warmest regards,

Tom Bailey

Dear Mr Ure,
Other than within the privacy of an open space with no others present, I must urge you to refrain from dancing with tears in your eyes, given that the restricted vision associated with the blurring moisture is likely to endanger both yourself and others.

Dear Rick Astley,
I thank you for your concern but please be reassured that my heart has not been aching. In the event that it were, I can categorically confirm that I would most definitely NOT be too shy to say it, but would immediately consult a medical professional. A bashful demeanour could ultimately prove to be fatal.

Dear Baby Bird,
I am flattered, sir. If indeed you WOULD do anything for me, my garage guttering is in dire need of having the leaves picked out of it, but I need someone to hold the ladder and my son is away. Can we say Thursday at 3?

Dear Republica,

Re: Ready To Go

As you may be aware, the house opposite has just had a loft conversion done, which was sadly undertaken by a disreputable contractor, resulting in a profoundly fissured chimney breast, haphazard joists and a shoddily grouted dormer susceptible to complete de-glazing in the face of nothing more potent than an errant shuttlecock.

Once alerted, Bournemouth Borough Council inspectors conducted a thorough inspection of the discreditable garret and, horrified by their findings, insisted upon the ignominious sky parlour being fully ameliorated prior to building approval being granted. Unfortunately, rather than addressing the defects properly, the owners opted for a much more economical 'botch-job', which incorporated half a tub of Polyfilla and an unmatching Dulux Tester Pot in an attempted concealment of the aforementioned flue crevice.

It was with some dismay, but no little surprise therefore, that my wife Jean and I were awakened this morning by both her PC tablet alarm clock (tuned, obviously, to Bournemouth's peerless Wave 105.2 FM) and an almighty ruckus coming from across the road. Further investigation from a discreet gap in the curtains revealed that the officials had returned to the slapdash attic and, thoroughly unimpressed by the frugal and deceptive improvements undertaken, were now teetering precariously astride the tiles and pointing at the stack, angrily and loudly protesting at its deceptive restoration.

It was at this very juncture in the confrontational governing body/ extra storey owner proceedings that your 'techno-pop-punk classic' came on just after the travel; 'It's a crack, I'm back, yeah, standing on the rooftops shouting out', uncannily acting as an eerie narrative to the scene that we were witnessing at that very instant. There, however, any similarity ended; far from being 'ready to go', the furious officials seemed intent on maintaining their 'lofty' position until the matter could be resolved.

Notwithstanding this last incongruity, Jean and I remain extremely impressed by your local authority versus resident soundscaping abilities, although must take issue with your assertion that one week is another world; it is, in actuality, not a different planet but a seven day unit of time.

Finally, Jean has just suggested from the kitchen, where she is toasting a muffin, that in the current climate of so many establishments closing, you may be well advised to consider renaming your indie combo 'ReWineBarLica' or 'ReBeersAtHomeLica', in order to reflect current trends.

Yours,

Derek Philpott

....

Dear Derek,

I'm very sorry to hear that you and Jean have had to go through this harrowing situation which sounds at the very least drop dead dangerous! I know what it is like to have noisy neighbours as I am currently being woken up every morning by Bertie the mini Schnauzer from next door who seems to like barking at 5.30am. It is at this time every day I feel like 'I'm in another world', I can tell you!

I do hope the chim chim-in-ey people across the road have finally

completed the fissure on said breast and that there will be no more interruptions to Jean's muffin making.

Thank you so much for your tip regarding the 'Pub' in our name. From now on we will be billed as 'The Pubs' to reflect current trends as it is in fact our natural habitat. When we next do a show in Bournemouth it would be wonderful to meet you. I will bring cake.

Love and kindest regards,

Saffron The Pubs Poppins
xxx

Dear Elvis Costello and 'The Attractions',

In your eponymous 'new wave anthem', you state that 'Oliver's Army' are both on their way and here to stay.

As much as my wife Jean and I enjoy your innovative 'post-punk' sound, we must, however, admit to being confused as to the actual whereabouts of the informal battalion referred to therein. Given that they are 'on their way' – that is to say, yet to arrive, or were until recently present at your unknown destination and have just left – please advise as to precisely how said marauding troops could possibly be 'here to stay' at a point which has been specifically referred to as unsettled within during the time of writing.

Furthermore, as regards your claim that you 'would rather be anywhere else', an amendment in the 'lyric' to 'rather be in most other places' is required, given your mooted aversion, as alluded to elsewhere in your 'back catalogue', to The Borough Of Kensington and Chelsea.

Finally, given that the unit is referred to as a collective noun, Oliver's Army is on *its* way, surely, gentlemen.

We are also perplexed with regard to another declaration, vis-à-vis Every Day I Write The Book. Either one is to assume that a new tome is penned every 24 hours, or that, alternatively, you have been toiling upon the same project, which by your own admission boasts a mere six chapters, for some decades now. The former scenario suggests a work of dubious quality and a disappointed readership, the latter a severe case of writer's block and an exasperated publishing house. Until such time as a literary standard reflective of a realistically befitting time-frame or deadline can be mustered, a continued revenue stream generated by pop concerts and 'festival appearances' alone is to be recommended.

Finally, it is with regret that I must request the particulars of your management company and/or legal representatives. Against my better judgement and the manufacturer's guidelines detailed within the handbook in my glove compartment, and in accordance with your dubious instructions on Steve Wright (which I took to be borne of some pop star insider knowledge pertaining to this year's model), I pulled my Nissan Juke into the Murco at Southbourne Grove this afternoon. After popping into the kiosk for Quavers I then inflated my rear and front tyres to just shy of 52 psi, 22 and 19 in excess of the recommended 30 psi front/33 psi back already within them. Said over-bloating saw all four inner walls ruptured just before Undercover Boss Canada. In the case of each Michelin, to pump it up when I don't really need it has saddled me with an unwanted bill from my mechanic on The Nuffield Industrial Estate totalling £135 non-inclusive of VAT, which I insist upon being settled by your good selves without my resorting to civil proceedings. Whilst fully acknowledging that 'Accidents Will Happen', on this occasion I fail to see that all four explosions can be attributed to anything other than wanton and unqualified advice.

I bid you good day.

Yours,

Derek Philpott

PS 'My aim is true', you may claim, but my neighbour Wilf Turnbull is insistent that he spied a bespectacled gentleman and his three cohorts playing Crazy Golf in Boscombe Gardens last week, seemingly disproving this rather dishonest declaration; his putting was decidedly inaccurate, and at one point his wild approach shot on the fifth tee ended up in the pond after ricocheting off a miniature windmill.

....

Dear Mr Philpott,

I recently became aware of your letter to Elvis Costello and the Attractions. I'm sorry that your observations have so far elicited no reply from my erstwhile colleagues. I fear you may not be aware that his current supporting musicians are actually imposters – and I'm not even sure about yer man himself. While you await some official explanation, I am happy to try and illuminate matters for you. Consequently, and somewhat to my surprise, I now find myself in the uncustomary position of speaking up on Mr Costello's behalf!

Incidentally, on the same topic, you may equally well have tackled the late Mr John Lennon who wrote: 'And so this is Christmas. And what have you done? Another year over. And a new one just begun.' Here, the late Beatle songsmith has New Year already begun when he has just said that it's Christmas!

We need now to delve into the realms of esotericism in order to illustrate how events seemingly separated by time can co-exist ...

It was in his 1884 novel Flatland: A Romance of Many Dimensions that the Victorian schoolmaster Dr Edwin Abbott offered us a simple analogy to show how the nature of time is dependent on our perception of it. In Flatland, Abbott describes what life would be like in a Flat world inhabited by figures something like ink blots that can slide around within a sheet of paper. The social order of this Flat world was such that the geometrical figures with most sides ruled over those with fewer. The most powerful had so many sides that they looked almost like circles.

One day, Flatland is visited by a Sphere. So we can imagine the sense of mystery and wonder as such a being suddenly begins to materialize in this world, appearing first as a small circle that steadily increases in size as the Sphere manifests in Flatland in the only way that it can – as a cross-section.

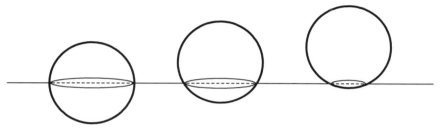

The Sphere moves in and out of the Flat world trying to demonstrate to the Flatlanders that there is a 3rd dimension of space. But all they see is a point that grows to a circle and then shrinks down again only to disappear. The Flat people can't understand that these different circles, appearing and disappearing at different times, all belong to the same body in a higher dimension — that all these circles belong to one body, a Sphere that is present all of the time!

What Abbott is saying, of course, is that we ourselves are no better off than Flatlanders when it comes to recognizing higher dimensions. But his example of the entry of the 3rd dimension of space into the 2nd is one that can help us to understand the 3rd dimension of time.

Now, suppose a pencil was to pass vertically through this Flat land, then, as with the Sphere, only a thin cross-section would actually exist in it. Remember, the paper beings know nothing else but their 'paper world' and what lies in it. So they would only ever see the cross-section of the pencil that lies within it. All the rest of the pencil would be invisible to them, even though it exists all-at-once in our world.

As the pencil passed through their world they would see only successive cross-sections. What has already appeared would now be invisible and belong to their 'past'. What hasn't yet appeared would be in their 'future'. It would be more like a series of events. They could never experience the pencil as an integrated whole or know that it had a form and purpose far beyond their imagining.

The scientists of Flatland could analyse the pencil, its chemical composition and so on until they believed they knew all about it – without ever looking for a higher explanation or realizing that their knowledge was only a very limited expression of a much greater reality.

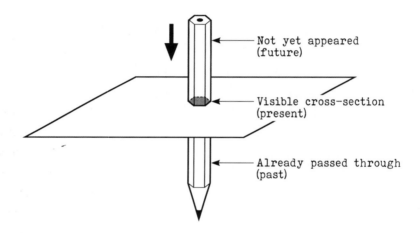

Just as the Flatlanders can only ever see a cross-section of space, so our own human senses only ever experience a 'slice of time'. It's as if we see life like a film being shown frame by frame, even though the whole story is there in the reel in the projector. We have no experience of the 3rd dimension of time, which extends into a dimension hidden from our ordinary senses, where everything is present.

In the Flat world, as the pencil begins to pass through the paper the Flatlanders first see only a point, and then the small circle of graphite that begins to grow around it, before growing a thick coating of wood. The process of growth in our own world is the same; we can think of the growth of a plant or a person from a 'seed' in just the same way. We can't make a plant or a person from a pile of chemicals; we can only watch them grow. This growth comes from a higher dimension that enters our world, over time, from a dimension where the entire plant – seed, bud, leaf, fruit – is present all at once.

The Flatlanders can only understand through their intuition and imagination what we can see naturally all the time. What we see with our senses they can only see in their imagination and insight. The analogy of Flatland says that we are no different. Just as the 2 dimensions of Flatland are contained in a 3rd dimension of space, so our own world exists in a higher, 3rd dimension of time. This 3rd dimension of time – this absolute whole of solid time – holds all possible pasts, presents and futures; everything that exists, has existed or could exist in any place, at any time. It means that, all at the same time, everything, everywhere, is present.

Our traditional idea of eternity is a false one. We usually think of time as an arrow coming out of the distant past progressing towards an equally distant future. And we assume that this thrust is somehow connected with 'evolution', 'civilization' or 'progress'. The eternal life of religion pictures it as going on 'for ever and ever... Amen'. All of these views are based on the idea of time as a kind of an endless one-way street. But just as a line extended infinitely into space can never produce a square or a cube, so a line in time will never reach eternity.

Paul Davies, professor of Theoretical Physics, University of Newcastle, says: 'I am often asked what happened before the Big Bang. The answer is that there was no 'before', because the Big Bang represents the appearance of Time itself. People say "something must have caused it". But cause and effect are concepts of time and cannot be applied to a state where time doesn't exist. The question is meaningless. "Time, as we know it, begins with and emerges from the same source as the universe," said St Augustine.'

So in the matter of the co-existence of all time, even religion and science agree! In eternity everything is present; we can't ask what happened before creation as it would imply creation happened in some remote past of passing-time. The universe wasn't made in time, but is made with time. In the process of creation, time itself is created. There can be nothing 'before' time; we can only say that there is time. And in Time, everything exists, all at the same time.

I hope this goes some way towards explaining how Oliver's Army can be on their way at the same time that they are here today. As regards your other observations, rather than address these at this present time (I could of course address them at some 'future' present time) I think we might both need to put the kettle on and crack open a packet of Mint Viscounts.

Yours respectfully,

Bruce Thomas

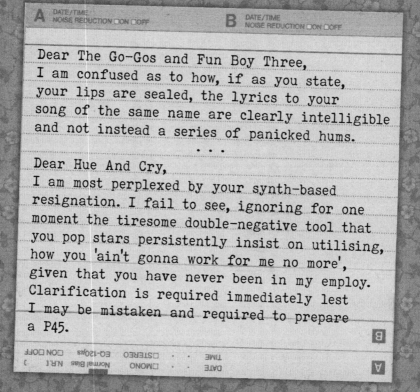

Dear The Go-Gos and Fun Boy Three,
I am confused as to how, if as you state, your lips are sealed, the lyrics to your song of the same name are clearly intelligible and not instead a series of panicked hums.

. . .

Dear Hue And Cry,
I am most perplexed by your synth-based resignation. I fail to see, ignoring for one moment the tiresome double-negative tool that you pop stars persistently insist on utilising, how you 'ain't gonna work for me no more', given that you have never been in my employ. Clarification is required immediately lest I may be mistaken and required to prepare a P45.

Dear Jona Lewie,

Re: You'll Always Find Me In The Kitchen At Parties

I recently heard you state on Top of the Pops 2 that you are no good, on account of always getting rebuffed, at chatting up. You added that this is enough to drive a man, referring almost certainly to yourself, to drink, and that you are also averse to washing up, but I will always find you in the kitchen at parties.

Throughout my life I have attended many social gatherings, from anniversaries, birthdays and charity fundraisers to the 'leaving do' of my erstwhile work compadre Willy 'Won't He' Wallace and the 'wrap bash' of an ITV 'situation comedy' that I was allowed into because the father of one of my son's friends was one of the show's 'schoolchildren' in it at the time.

I can categorically confirm, Mr Lewie, that I have never encountered your good self in the food preparation area of any of these jamborees, the closest namesake being a John Lewis teatowel on a draining board at a 50th which I have deduced must be extraneous on the grounds of your frowzy aversion to post-meal asepsis, as languidly imparted within your above-adduced 'Sprechgesang synthpop number'.

Didactically speaking, even were I to happen upon you in even one culinary area, such a singular congress could not in any way be construed as interminable.

By your own admission, Mr Lewie, you have taken assuagement in alcohol as a means of contending with latent courtier-spurnings causatum of exiguous *savoir faire*, and if you will exculpate my bumptiousness, your increasing dipsomania seems sadly to have addled you to the extent that you now believe yourself to have been a draftee in manifold conflicts hundreds of years apart. Thankfully for your fellow combatants, your befuddled misapprehension is delusionary. Were this not to be the case, should your feeble appeals to the Prime

Minister regarding your dragoon cessation prove successful, I would be extremely concerned about the morale deflation and detrimental psychological effects caused to your colleagues on the front line, just so *you* can spend the festive period at home.

I would also sincerely hope that you would not attempt to alleviate the repressive atmosphere of your predicament by ensconcing yourself in the cooking zone of a 'mess' (not to be confused with the myriad of pots, pans and plates that you so resolutely refuse to rinse) whose regiment you have persuaded to partake in raucous merry-making. I would ask you to remember, Mr Lewie, that in a battle situation, complete silence when approaching or in auditory range of the foe is paramount in order to avoid the inevitability of giving one's position away to said enemy.

On a lighter note, my wife Jean and I, accompanied by our neighbours Wilf and Olive Turnbull and Gordon and Nora Gillard, went for a most enjoyable Sunday lunch at a highly popular family 'eatery' on Christchurch Road last weekend. After a few too many 'Toby Tasters', followed by generously piling my plate high on no less than three visits to the heated buffet, Gordon asked me if I had room for one more sitting. I replied that, on the contrary, I was quite happy for them to 'Stop The Carvery'!

Although I wish you luck with your new album, I will thank you to avoid the inclusion of further 'New Wave Rock' glorifying crapulence-induced slovenly housekeeping and/or court martialable offences, for people to dance to in 'a new way'.

Yours,

Derek Philpott

Dear Derek (and Wilf),

Thank you for this opportunity to indulge in the dying art of writing a letter which is becoming a dim relic of a previous society.

In reply to your letter we could argue that, whether we are on the seafront, in the trenches or at a social gathering, I could recommend certain stuffs should be entered into the body in order that the promotion of health and happiness in one's life may be facilitated. For example:

1. Beetroot
2. Raw Garlic
3. Tomatoes
4. Broccoli
5. Plus many more items

We could also enclose soft salmon and soft fillet steak if you don't mind images of the poor cow or fish being slaughtered and then absorbed into your body; though at least by taking such protein your own protein is guaranteed a further tenure of existence before it again starts to crave more protein. Tofu, on the other hand, is one of various stuffs that can be used by those offended who feel staunchly for the poor beasts.

Not too recommended in the very long term view would be assuagement by alcohol. Water is a good Adam's wine and is permissible, even though Prime Minister Churchill quite rightly claimed that he got more out of alcohol than alcohol got out of him.

Not to be too Spartan or a spoilsport, we would not be enamoured with enticing sugars, though dark or black chocolate is useful (but not as necessary as Adam's Wine). One would also NOT take with a pinch of salt the notion that too much salt is dangerous to the mortal body.

Eating the right food stuffs in the kitchen, it can be suggested, will make for less need of trenches or the manufacture of cannon, rifles, torpedoes and other weapons, some of which are well known (for example, nuclear bombs). This is because the right food stuffs can encourage the right moods which are of an anti-belligerent nature. Amen and God Save America, plus all the other countries.

With regards to your letter and on a final note, I can reassure you that topics from the next album will go beyond the kitchen and the fallout zone in order to look at tears and joy derived from other soups and sauces, of which there are indeed plenty.

Take good care,

Jona Lewie

Dear The Mock Turtles,

I am most grateful to you, The Mock Turtles.

It was a particularly pleasant day today, of which my wife Jean and I took full advantage by having lunch on the patio with our neighbours Wilf and Olive Turnbull, accompanied by the splendid Ken Bruce on Radio 2 through an open window. As it was one of very few forays past the conservatory doors for some time on account of a rather dismal winter, we were sadly afforded only the first opportunity to observe the extent to which our garden had become overrun with brambles. After a second pot of Earl Grey and one too many Orange Viscounts, and whilst pondering the most effective method of loosening the sun-hardened soil at the roots of said unwanted vegetation, Wilf proffered several suggestions. He asked if I could 'rotavate' it – sadly not an option owing to a blown fuse – and then could I try a trowel, as he was confident that I would get it through somehow. This proved ineffective, however, owing to insufficient leverage and a clay-encrusted blade after too long unscraped which did little more than crumble the surface layer, rendering our intrusive perennial steadfast. Undecided as to our next option and fast becoming despondent, your excellent and persistent well-informed enquiry 'Can You Dig It?' sent me eagerly to the shed for my favoured spade, Lemmy, who eradicated the infestation with aplomb.

As well as your adroitness in horticultural matters, The Mock Turtles, I am sure that you will not mind me complimenting you upon your ecological sensibilities. I was extremely perturbed by Blondie's assertion on Top Of The Pops 2 last week that she will give me her finest hour, the one she spent watching me shower. Leaving aside that time cannot be bestowed and, given that it takes me a fraction of this time to cleanse upright, my bathroom or front doors show no signs of forced entry, leading me to conclude that I must have been confused for somebody else. Nevertheless, her glorification of such a grotesque waste of water in stark contrast to your insistence that 'someone turn the lights off' only serves to enhance your awareness of the importance pertaining to pop stars educating us ordinary members of the public in utility usage-helmed affairs of the environment.

I confess, The Mock Turtles, that ever since seeing Buddy Holly on television and expecting his other musicians to be nocturnal grasshopper-like insects but finding them in actuality more redolent of three trainee bank managers, I have been unwaveringly fascinated by 'band names'. As an animal lover, I was dreading, in your own case, that the employment of the definitive article serves merely as a superfluous juxtaposition inserted as a subtle subterfuge designed to encourage people (subliminally or otherwise) to mock turtles and/or, by extension, tease terrapins. I was therefore initially relieved to learn that a mock turtle is *not* a shelled reptile ridicule reference, but in reality, a soup; then dismayed to glean that the liquid sustenance's stock ingredients are brains and organ meats – including the head and foot of a calf, branding it as a baby cow production.

If only your endorsement of such a cruel liquid mélange could have been reconciled by your agrological expertise and admirable 'carbon footprint', you would have been welcome at any time here at Philpott Place for tea on the newly-unimpeded decking.

Until such time, we are equally confident that we won't ever get you down and congratulate you upon your continued and perpetual buoyancy.

Kind Regards

Yours,

Derek Philpott

....

Dear Derek (and Wilf),

It appears that you distinguished and learned gentlemen have, like myself, a proclivity for calling a spade an 'earth-inverting horticultural implement', and why not? For language is the shed of tools in the garden of life itself and we are in the full harvest reaping pure gold. I am glad my little horticultural ditty gave you the inspiration needed in the battle of the bramble and should the need arise whereby a gardening problem occurs requiring musical intervention, please feel free to call on me for a bespoke melodious solution.

I doff my cap to you both in admiration.

Yours,

Martin from The Mock Turtles

Dear It's Immaterial,

Re: Driving Away From Home

My wife Jean and I are most intrigued by your 'Sprechgesang smash', and feel there to be some 'mileage' in attempting to elicit some 'Kind Words' from you in response to several queries that I have compiled. 'Is That Alright?'

Assuming so, I am somewhat aghast that you should instruct your designated driver to just get in, close the door and put their foot down, which is to be assumed to refer to initiating instantaneous acceleration. Forgive my suggesting, my unpertinent correspondees, that 'The Better Idea' may have been to ensure that both the unnamed motorist and all passengers – especially children and infants, if applicable – were ensured to have had all of their seat belts securely fastened, and that Section 2, paragraph 163 of The Highway Code (more colloquially recognised as 'Mirrors, Signal, Manoeuvre') was observed prior to setting off, at speed, from a kerb 'In The Neighbourhood'.

It should also be considered that, not unlike your 'band name', the appendation of 'or more' to a thirty mile boundary reference, thus disestablishing an apical parameter to it, renders said quoted distance extraneous. Put simply, the voiding of an upper ambit limit does somewhat despecify and therefore invalidate the detailing of any range whatsoever.

Moreover, 'Heaven Knows' how many times I have been late for an engagement on account of relying on the estimated arrival time displayed by my 'sat nav', which has rather optimistically surmised that there would be no roadworks, low bridge to high juggernaut impediments, 'school runs' or floodings at any point of my journey. Therefore, unless of course one's device is able to connect to the internet and draw on live traffic data, to state in the public forum of the pop charts that it is only thirty nine miles and forty five minutes to Manchester, especially when ignorant of the audience's current location at the time of listening to 'Your Voice', could be construed as both presumptuous and misleading.

Finally, It's Immaterial, although many of us with 'An Ordinary Life' only own one property, there are others (including, until recently, MPs, for whom the second home allowance was scrapped in 2011, resulting no doubt in numerous 'House For Sale' signs) who have more. For this particular section of society, 'Driving Away From One Home But Towards Another' would surely be a more accurate, if admittedly less hummable 'offering'.

On a lighter note, my wife Jean is very keen to learn more about the shop that you like where you can get anything. Even her favourite retailer, Beales on Old Christchurch Road, as varied and all-encompassing as it is, still lacks next week's Lotto Rollover numbers, twenty years off her age, and world peace.

I remain yours sincerely,

Derek Philpott

....

Dear Mr P and Jean,

Thank you for your correspondence which I received the other day and have since been ruminating over. Your deep slice research into my back catalogue seems to have thrown up a number of counts on which you hold issues, particularly pertaining to the title Driving Away From Home. Allow me to attempt clarification.

I take on board your reservations with regard to my invitation once in the vehicle for the driver to 'put your foot down'; in hindsight this might sound more like the instruction of an accomplice to a getaway driver. I believe in this case it must have been the muse that led me to neglect health and safety concerns at the time and if ever I was to

make a revision, I would probably open the piece as follows: 'Just get in and check your mirror, if all's clear select first gear'.

Now let's consider, as you put it, the appendation of 'or more' to the thirty miles stated. The said thirty miles was merely a suggestion as to the minimum ground you might wish to cover to make the whole journey worth your while cerebrally, otherwise one might as well 'just as well nip down the shops'. I added the 'or more' so as not to cage the driver's enthusiasm to burn rubber or as I should say (with health and safety now firmly in mind) drive with due care and attention.

As for your suggested alternative title of 'Driving Away From One Home To Another', it has merit and to ignore the potentially lucrative market of the second home owner was an oversight at the time and is something I will look into further down the road.

By the way – that shop, it's on the road to Wigan.

Regards,

Mr It's Immaterial

Dear Mr. McNabb,

Re: Love Is A Wonderful Colour

I regret, sir, that the song that you have 'penned' for performance by your functioning sharp-pointed frozen water monickered 'combo' requires not inconsiderable critical scrutiny.

Prior to being exposed to your sprightly composition this morning I must admit never to having considered that, to directly quote from the work, 'love is full of wonderful colours', and I am admittedly still quite perplexed as to precisely how such feelings of overwhelming fondness are able to be so marvellously and chromatically engorged.

As you may or may not be aware, Mr McNabb, 'colour' is nothing more than the admittedly quite spectacular result of electromagnetic hue cycle and retinal interaction. It is, by this very definition, a process, and therefore unable to substantially occupy ardour, which is itself devoid of both dimension and structure.

In conclusion then, and pending verifiable evidence to the contrary, I regret to inform you that the central premise of the piece, coupled with the observation that feelings of romantic attachment are also a luminous device specifically designed to draw attention to a perceived point at which the earth and sky converge (i.e. 'a beacon on the horizon'), is, unfortunately, wholly untenable.

Aside from the above correction, I hope you will forgive me for noticing that you appear to have an aversion against or hostility towards various forms of arboreal matter. This is clear from the inescapable fact that by your own admission, adjacent to some burning wood, you appear to have been engrossed in conversation to the extent that the blazing structural tissue (possibly the result of faulty wiring in an outbuilding or shed) evinces little to no concern. Furthermore, another of your pop songs, Chop The Tree, brazenly encourages the more suggestible listener to fell all manner of large bark-enclosed plants without prior verification of the presence or absence of disease, qualification as an endangered species, jurisdiction or otherwise under the National Trust, and/or permission of the landowner in whose property the condemned topiary stands. I must recommend that your obvious timber-based vendetta ceases forthwith.

I hope that you do not object to the points made within this missive and would like to assure you that my wife Jean and I are keen enthusiasts of your output. I hope that you will not mind but I must now take leave of my computer in order to attend to a puncture and badly worn rear brake pad for my son. With luck, once the repairs have been successfully completed, I will be able to report that the bicycle works!

Please accept my apologies for the pun above.

Yours sincerely,

Derek Philpott

··

Dear Mr Philpott,

**Thank you for your letter. I do have to say though that I have often
dreaded the long overdue in-depth analysis of this song, the more
famous of my two entries into the UK top forty singles chart (the
other being Let The Young Girl Do What She Wants To which I
hope you will avoid critiquing due to its relative obscurity), as I
myself have been troubled by the lyrics for over thirty years now.**

**If it has annoyed anyone due to its clumsy, nonsensical, random
pseudo-psychedelic lyric, may I put forth that, as irritating as it is,
you the listener have not had to sing it on stage for the last 30 years.
If I had been aware at the time of how long this ditty would endure
in the hearts of music enthusiasts the world over, I would have spent
a bit more time on it. I do think you got off lightly, however, as the
original title for this slab of Phil Spector-inspired pop was 'My Heart
Belongs To A Frozen Lake', so bear in mind that, however bad things
are, they could always be a lot worse.**

**In the eighties (a time much maligned in memory by the many,
but for the few it was a glorious time of hit albums and endless
world tours) it was a lot easier to get away with nonsense lyrics, as
a perusal through many of my contemporaries' works will attest.
Killing moons and kissing tortoise shells was all the rage at the time.
My cruel treatment of wood during this period is a moot point and
I hold my hands up to abusing it on a number of occasions, albeit
only in verse. Track one on the debut Icicle Works long player has
me instructing the listener to 'Chop The Tree' and by track two I
appear to be talking to a friend as we both presumably sit beside**

some 'burning wood'. I have no idea what any of this means and cannot even claim to be influenced by burning other substances in order to arrive at this maniacal wanton abuse of trees, as at the point the songs were conceived I was still a three pints of lager man.

Finally, my abstract metaphor instructing folk that 'Love Is A Wonderful Colour' is nothing more than disguised theft of the title 'Love Is Such A Beautiful Place' a song by fellow Liverpudlian songsmith Michael Head, then of the band Pale Fountains. Thank you for publicly admonishing my lyrical and green crimes; it has given me cause for thought and I hereby promise to be a little kinder to forests (and myself) in future.

Sincerely,

Ian McNabb

Dear Go West,
You state in your jaunty hit that an unnamed young female should not look down given that she knows she is holding aces. Forgive me saying that the awareness of possession of a particularly strong selection of playing cards does not negate one from protecting oneself against a potentially lethal fall into a crevice or over the edge of a cliff.

Dear Ms Ellis-Bextor,
Allow me to assure you that in the event of witnessing a murder on the dancefloor I would most certainly 'kill the groove'. I would also insist that nobody be permitted to leave the premises until all names and addresses of those in attendance have been recorded. I am also concerned that you yourself are a potential 'perp' given that you intend to burn the goddamned house right down, thereby destroying all forensic evidence pertaining to this heinous crime.

Dear Matt Bianco,
Re: Get Out Of Your Lazy
Bed. I am confused,
Mr Bianco. Surely it is
the encumbent and not
the framework itself that
is slothful?

Mr Rodgers,
I fear that the lady
smiling from her head to
her feet is not in need of
a kiss, but urgent medical
attention to repair her
severe jaw dislocation.

Dear Howard Jones,

Re: Like To Get To Know You Well

I am flattered but surprised, Mr Jones, at your direct and rather forward approach. I have discussed the matter with my wife Olive, and we have decided that you would be a welcome visitor 'chez Turnbull', on the following condition:

> That you abandon the practice of keeping your body-popping sidekick chained up in a box, only to emerge during your musical offerings, such as the above.

As you may be aware, slavery was abolished in all British territories in 1834, and it is certainly 'bad form' for potential acquaintances to indulge in such practice. It is perhaps ironic that you urge your listeners to 'throw off your mental chains, woo-hoo-hoo' during the admittedly catchy 'New Song', while simultaneously coaxing a servile performance from your gimp-like captive.

However, once you assure us that your cohort is treated as an equal, you will be warmly welcomed.

In answer to your enquiry 'What is Love?' I am able to inform you that it can be defined as 'an intense emotion of affection, warmth, fondness and regard towards a person or thing'. As I appear to have mislaid his address, please could you forward this information to 'Haddaway', who I believe has recently formed a duo with Dieter Scheidt, the well-known Austrian DJ.

I hold your musical output in high regard, Mr Jones, and look forward to your response. I would also like to know of any special dietary requirements you have, and request that you provide us with a reasonable period of notice. Please note that Wednesday evenings are inconvenient. In addition, perhaps it would be possible to bring your marvellous 'electronic keyboard', and give an informal concert after tea in our living room, although the sideboard will need to be relocated.

Yours sincerely,

Wilf Turnbull

....

Dear Mr Turnbull,

I am most pleased with your decision to make me welcome at Chez Turnbull and to 'aimez faire connaissance avec vous bien'. However, the conditions you propose are most unwelcome. We live in an age of freedom of expression and I feel to burden Mr Hoile with the weight of your shallow cultural preferences could prove to be an obstacle beyond my ability to transcend.

Mr Hoile (or Jed, as he is affectionately known) is the willing instrument of analogy and a true champion of the art of Mental Chain unburdening. To cast him as oppressed or even marginally demeaned fills my heart with a nagging ache that I fear will not easily be cured by silver-tongued monologues or indeed efficacious herbs.

As for the question ancienne, ce qui est l'amour? I can only reveal that a young Master Haddaway was spotted, in disguise of course, at one of my concerts in New York in the mid 80s. I can only speculate

on the benign influence that may have occurred, and of course take a tiny modicum of pride in the progeny of that cause.

Casting all aside and looking to the future, I am indeed thrilled to be able to commit to next Saturday afternoon at 3pm. My keyboard Butler will arrive at 1pm to supervise the installation of my 'Circus Electronique' and cup cakes decorated with the names of keyboard legends (Tomita, Vangelis, Les Dawson) would suit my dietary obsessions quite nicely.

Regards to Olive,

Howard Jones

Dear Public Image Limited,

Re: This Is Not A Love Song

Although I have never run my own business working all the hours that God sends, Public Image Limited, I have over the years encountered many ceaselessly toiling company directors that have; normally in pubs in the early afternoon leading continuously into the late evening. The most prosperous of these 'self-made men' has undoubtedly been Gerald Nagle from The Baker's Arms in Lychett Minster, who back in 1983 struck upon the novel idea of supplying high quality second-hand yachts, luxury cars and helicopters to the more affluent residents of Sandbanks and the surrounding areas.

Following a visit to the florist's earlier this week for our wedding anniversary, I decided, upon the consideration that Jean might have wanted chocolates instead, to assuage myself with a half a Tetley's. It was during this consolatory libation that I played said impresario your 'post-punk smash' on the jukebox, 'PiL', whilst joking that together with Placebo you would be more grammatically suited to be played on a 'tablet'.

I hope that you will not mind my relating that after the 'fade out' was replaced by Save All Your Kisses For Me, my co-listener merely frowned and stated that were 'Floaters Rotors & Motors' to adopt a similar campaign, its success in the commercial zone would likely be severely compromised on the basis that negatory detraction in big business is very *unwise*. I must admit that his illustratory example of a used E65 7 Series BMW being ambiguously marketed as 'This Is Not A Mercedes-Benz CLK-class Cabriolet', thus potentially aggravating the prospective purchaser whilst neglecting to advertise any Unique Selling Points of the vehicle on offer, was most compelling, as was his utter exasperation at the failure of a trader whose brand name literally reflected its recognition of a strong civil profile to be conscious of said faux pas.

Furthermore, the concept of 'television behind the curtain' in any feasibility whatsoever was anathema to him, he added. It is crucial for all wares featured on the screen of a plastic and/or 'metal box' to be unobscured by shrouding drapery in order that the 'Album' of products available may be clearly visible. He is also at a loss as to why one may be asked if one is 'ready to grab the candle, not television'. Not only is potential wick grippage probably hazardous; to the best of our knowledge there is no facility to display photographs via the medium of an illuminatory wax block.

Please 'Don't Ask Me' to desist from availing you of the above observations, or be 'Disappointed' by Gerald's appraisal, Public Image Limited. Sadly 'This Is What You Get' when scrutinised by your enterprising peers. He could be wrong, he could be right. I am sure that you will 'Rise' above it and refocus your corporation to a more and nonfilthy lucrative income stream in the near future, near future, near future for you.

Yours,

Derek Philpott

Dear Mr Philpott,

Many thanks for your recent communiqué addressed to Public Image Limited regarding their (only) chart topping smash hit This Is Not A Love Song. On behalf of all employees of the corporation, past and present, may I declare the greatest appreciation for your time and utmost dedication in giving the lyrics of the aforementioned song your careful consideration.

I must stress from the outset that I am replying to your letter very much in the capacity of an ex-employee of the corporation having myself resigned in 1983; Lord Johnny Fartpants of Islington is currently unavailable, being as he is rather busy these days, diligently making butter adverts, appearing in second rate reality TV shows or generally buffooning around on daytime television and radio promoting his recent poorly written tome. However, I am sure he, along with other revered ex-employees such as Mr Atkins and my dearest friend Mr Levene, would concur with the sentiments I have expressed in this letter.

May the corporation also take this opportunity to extend the heartiest of congratulations to you and your good wife Jean on your recent wedding anniversary. I think buying her flora that can only be described as 'Flowers of Romance' was a particularly good and fitting idea. It seems that Jean is a remarkable woman and is clearly the backbone of the Philpott household. She must have remarkable patience and fortitude to stand by you as you spend countless hours hunched over your electronic device tapping out witty retorts to various (fading) rock stars.

So, with the pleasantries duly dispensed with, let us turn to the points you raised most eloquently in your letter. I must say the letter was written with some remarkable aplomb; the many references to the corporation's work was (as many people have expressed that you should be) particularly well executed. Bravo!

The commercial success of the song in question is well documented, reaching – as it did in many other territories – the upper echelons of the UK pop charts. It remains a popular tune to this day, receiving regular airplay on what you may know as 'the wireless' and other media outlets that may be less familiar to a gentleman of your years. The song in fact still remains a contributor to my meagre musician's royalty income, not bad for half a day's work 33 years ago! You will know of course through your own due diligence that no other PiL releases before or since have reached the same giddy heights of chart success.

As to the specific lyrical content of the said song; 'TV behind the curtain' is clearly, by today's programme listings that are full of poor quality programmes, the best place to put it… pure genius!

And 'grabbing the candle' is very sound advice in my honest opinion (you may abbreviate this to IMHO in today's common on-line parlance if you wish). Candles should always be held quite firmly as any looseness of grip may find the candle falling from the hand and causing at worst a fire, or at best a nasty burn. Particularly good advice for the elderly! Wax spillages are also terribly difficult to remove from expensive Wilton carpets or those Draylon furniture covers favoured by pensioners.

Another line from the song, 'Big business is very wise', is one of the key phrases that Mr Lydon warbles in the song, and should be a reminder to fans and casual commentators such as yourselves that 'we know better than you'. As Mr Lydon continues to whine, 'better to have, not to have not'… sagacious advice indeed.

We do all hope that Mr Nagle remains successful, as he sounds just as remarkable a leader as our own beloved CEO, though I am sure he no longer frequents The Baker's Arms as it is now part of an awful gastropub chain, some reviews of which are, alas, unfavourable. The pub, rather like Public Image Limited, appears a former shadow of its 1983 self, despite the current employees and clientele.

I do hope I have dealt with your correspondence in an appropriate and decorous manner and all that remains is on behalf of the 45 or so employees of the corporation (41 of whom sadly have been made redundant over the years) to wish you well for 2015 and hope you manage to enjoy the little time you have left. Should you come into personal contact with dear Mr Lydon, do please pass on my gratitude and thanks for all he has done for my career over the years and at the same time, please ask 'When can I expect to get paid?'

Warmest regards,

Pete Jones
Chief bass operator, Department S

✕

Dear Mr Hucknall,
I am horrified to learn that you want to fall from the stars, straight into my arms. If one were inclined to drop an American penny from the top of the Empire State Building, the tumbling coin (assuming a weight of 2.5 grams if it were The Lincoln Memorial Reverse penny, manufactured from mid-1982 to the present), ignoring air resistance, would, assuming its landing point to be 1m above the ground and based upon the loose change exerting a kinetic average force of 79 pounds, bore a 1cm deep hole into the object or person upon impact. The 102 floor observatory is 145m tall, and the nickel and alloy circle quite light, as above-stated, but still the results are grisly. You are therefore unwelcome to plunge towards my limbs through space and I will most certainly be walking jerkily waving my limbs around in a haphazard fashion should I ever learn of an attempt. Having launched yourself, and although weightless before you bludgeon your way through our atmosphere which is 62 miles above ground, your rotund form, Hucknall, would exert about eighteen tons at terminal velocity. Thankfully for me, you are likely to evaporate upon re-entry.

Dear The Members,

Re: Sound of The Suburbs

As much as my wife Jean and I enjoy doing the washing up to your 'angsty anthem', which we found last night in the attic featured on a 'compilation CD' of the same name, one fears that the hubbub referenced therein may be atypical of most conventional city outskirt brouhaha.

It is to be conceded, The Members, that an old man washing his car, your mum in the kitchen cooking Sunday dinner, and a woman next door just sitting and staring outside are not abnormal peripheral metropolitan activities as exercised by 'Normal People' per se. One does struggle, however, unless he is using a particularly noisy hose and both ladies and their immediate environs are, to use a technical term no doubt familiar to you pop stars, 'heavily mic'd up', to comprehend how said perpetrations may in any way be provincially audible.

Furthermore, unless of course you are referring to a Crowthorne-based woman known to lure nearby sailors to their deaths, one finds it difficult to conceive as to how it may be possible to be individually pestered by mechanical warning circuitry. Are you absolutely certain that a Broadmoor siren won't leave you alone?

On a marginally non-germane note, I am slightly confused that you ask Johnny, who stands at his window at the night, what he is listening to, when to visually observe does not necessarily require stimuli discernible to the human ear.

All told, sirs, your humble correspondent, representing, I am confident, 'We The People', feels justified in declaring that until a full explanatory reply is forthcoming, 'These Are The Unresolved Issues Of The Suburbs'.

I remain yours sincerely,

Derek Philpott

PS Jean wonders, with regard to your erstwhile 'lead singer' Nicky Tesco, if he has any children, and if so, does he refer to any of the little ones as Tesco Express?

....

Dear Mr Philpott,

Re: These Are The Unresolved Issues Of The Suburbs

Looking at the lyrics to Sound of the Suburbs and seeing your analysis sent me spinning back in a vortex to 1978 when the original idea for the song entered my head. I shall address your concerns as to the 'flawed logic' of the lyrical content of the song later on in my communication but first I must 'set the scene' as it were for this song…

At the time the artistic movement called punk rock was in its infancy and there was a popular misconception that it was an urban movement that was the property of a small coterie of inner city 'cool kids', art students, fashionistas and the like. However, I noticed at the time that lots of youngsters from the outskirts of London began to attend our concerts. I saw in these fans two things: hunger for something different and the urgent desire to escape from what all teenagers see as a mundane life at home with their parents. These same teenagers had of course been brought up watching television where the frequent message was city = glamour and excitement; suburbs = boring. Some of them even wore their suburban dullness with pride and fashioned badges with the names of the depressing little hamlets they came from: 'Hampton Crew' (Mike Lacey, Neville Topping), 'Edgware Crew', etc. If I may paraphrase the late great Whitney Houston, I too believe that children are our future and at the time believed that these kids were actually in the ascendancy – they bought records and it was them who represented the majority of the UK as opposed to the aforementioned inner city cool kids. Ergo, I set about the task of writing them an anthem, a hymn to the mundanity they came from.

I was well suited to this task as my formative years were spent in a hamlet called Lightwater in Surrey, a place so impossibly unremarkable it made nearby Camberley seem like a metropolitan centre of the highest sophistication. Now I have set the scene, I will address your concerns as to the lyrical content of this song.

I take your point that washing a car and cooking dinner are not particularly noisy occupations. This nascent grammar schoolboy poet was trying to convey the impression that the 'sound of the suburbs' was the sound of 'nothing' because there was nothing happening. In short I tried to set a quiet scene so the punk rock electric guitar could explode through the monotony, complete with Heathrow jets roaring overhead and the ubiquitous Broadmoor siren.

I am sad to say that although I did for a short time have a girlfriend in nearby Sandhurst, the siren was not the Crowthorne femme fatale you allude to but a mechanical device similar to an air raid siren used to warn the people of Crowthorne and Camberley that an inmate had escaped from what a less politically correct world called a maximum security prison for the criminally insane, aka Broadmoor Hospital. This siren was tested without fail every Monday morning; its sound was clearly audible and impossible to block out and during my growing up years provided me with a regular and inescapable reminder of where I lived.

So there we are. In my defence I submit that these 'unresolved issues of the suburbs' are in part schoolboy poetic licence and the complicated mixing of 'sound' with metaphors.

All this artistic endeavour would have been impossible without the charismatic leadership and songwriting skill of Mr Nick Tesco and the dogged enthusiasm of other Members, to wit Mr Chris Payne, Mr Nigel Bennett and the (many are called but few are chosen) drummers that have honoured The Members' drum seat which is currently occupied by Mr Nick Cash (his real name and whose name was in part inspiration for the lead singer's re-christening as Nick Tesco). And to answer your good wife Jean, Nick Tesco does have children, though he is more inclined to refer to them as Tesco Excess than Express.

I hope this communication finds you as it leaves me in Excellent Rude Health.

JC Carroll
West Byfleet

Dear Anvil,

My wife Jean runs a small cottage industry called Philpottery from our home, making clay pop star animal fridge magnets such as Lady BudgeriGaGa, James HetField Mouse, Lion Tatler, ChimpanZZTop, Piggy Stardust, Nine Inch Snails, Swanny Rotten, Sharc Bolan, Axolotl Rose, Sheep Trick and Cheetah Gabriel.

Up until yesterday she was running the business from a dining tray on her lap on our sofa. However, after Moose Dickinson's antlers came off when she got up quickly to answer the phone and, inspired by listening to you at that very moment on Spotify, we resolved to invest in a self assembly IKEA stainless steel work table. Our decision was primarily based on listening to one of your 'pre-thrash crowd pleasers', on the assumption that a 'Metal On Metal' nuts, bolts and alloy construct would be both light and sturdy and help 'stop me' putting my back out when lifting.

Sadly, far from being what I craved, many difficulties were encountered when putting it together. The legs were uneven, which, instead of achieving stability, made it keep on rocking, keep on rocking, and

I distinctly remember getting quite angry when trying to manually screw a wingnut into a fiddly right angle to hear you correctly observe that thumbs will twist.

In the end, we had no option but to return the half-finished item to the retailer and exchange it for a more practical (if less aesthetically pleasing) alternative, of which there were many.

With this in mind, and in order that others may not feel the grind that Jean and I have experienced, we would be most grateful to hear a re-recorded version as soon as possible, entitled possibly 'Timber on Timber', 'MDF on MDF' or 'Hardboard on Plywood', as soon as possible.

Yours,

Derek Philpott

....

Dear Derek,

Great to hear from you.

Sorry to hear you have had difficulties with your Ikea decision....

'WHEN CHAINS OF DEATH HAVE BEEN UNLEASHED'.. with furniture assembly tasks, make sure you don't cut yourself leaving 'BLOOD ON THE ICE'....and always remember buying at Ikea you always 'PAY THE TOLL' along with you 'GET WHAT YOU PAID FOR'......'DON'T YOU WORRY, DON'T YOU SWEAT......I HAVE A METHOD THEY HAVEN'T THOUGHT OF YET'.....'WHEN DAMN NATION HAS BEGUN'.....

Read the ****ing instructions or you ain't got a 'HOPE IN HELL'!

Best,

Anvil

Dear The Alabama 3,

I write as a matter of urgency.

It is my normal custom upon rising after a good night's sleep to start the day with a bowl of Bran Flakes and a cup of Earl Grey. Today, however, I was dismayed to find upon opening the cupboard that the carton was fourteen days past its sell-by date, the exceeded high-fibre consumption deadline going some way to solving the mystery of nigh on a week's worth of soggy breakfasts. Deciding against the only other option in the house, namely my wife Jean's rather staid (in my opinion) Quaker Oats So Simple, I opted to turn the irksome situation to my advantage by popping into Café Riva on Overcliff Road and treating myself to a read of the Daily Express, a double espresso and a toasted teacake.

Imagine therefore my considerable alarm and discountenance upon settling my bill and turning to hear your 'Country Rave Offering' at the start of a programme on the television behind the counter about an opera singer driving to work. Not only had you (through means unknown) been somehow tracking my movements since I roused, which is unsettling enough, but your lead singer, The Very Reverend Dr D Wayne Love, was now without my permission incorrectly proclaiming your covert findings for all to hear. Most distressing of all, his gravelly misenunciation was extremely likely to result in our living room, which my wife Jean is particularly rigorous in keeping tidy, being severely disarrayed in the near future.

This is hardly the standard of behaviour expected of a man of the cloth.

To be perfectly clear, The Alabama 3, I woke up this morning and got myself a *bun*. I must therefore insist that if you must pursue your directive of advertising my daily errands to all and sundry, and in order that a warrant to search Philpott Place is not issued on the grounds of suspected contravention of Section 1 of The Firearms Act 1968, your 'propulsive hip-hop staple' be removed from the public domain or veraciously re-recorded immediately upon receipt of this missive.

Although I am less concerned with regard to a further oversight vis-à-vis your assumption that I was born under a bad sign (I am in actual fact a Libran; intuitive and fair, according to Russell Grant), I can fully understand how one may be cursed, being put in mind of a young lady whose waters broke beneath a tattoo parlour in Bournemouth recently, which bore the placard 'Ears Pearced While U Wait'.

I look forward to your prompt action in resolving the sorry matter above-mentioned and sincerely hope that this can be achieved amicably without recourse to a civil action.

Yours,

Derek Philpott

PS With regard to your pop group name, I was intrigued to discover through the perusal of a renowned 'online information tool' that you are neither Alabamian nor have the stated number of musicians in your 'lineup', and wonder whether, as a harmonious counterpoint, there exists in the relevant southeastern region of the United States a similar combo meeting both criteria known as The Brixton Nine. Also, given that your billing is often abbreviated to 'A3', whether this has at any time caused confusion when ordering posters at Prontaprint to publicise your 'Acid Hoedowns'.

....

Dear Mr Philpott,

It is with great concern that I reply to this missive. You are obviously labouring under delusions that a teacake is a bun.

According to The Health Food and Safety Regulation Act 1973, a teacake does not have self-raising flour in it.

A bun, according to the Act, is characterized by a self-raising flour constituent. It is so very disappointing in this day and age, to hear again another tragic story so indicative of the neglect into which we allow our older members to fall.

You have obviously been bereft of the appropriate legal advice and consequently, your heart-wrenching letter has elicited this response.

Your concern for out of date high-fibre content, and your wife's dependence on Oats So Simple, says so much about the issues that concern Alabama 3 vis-à-vis the staple diet of the elderly, and the failure of successive governments to address their breakfast issues adequately.

We hope that your abandonment of your wife Jean did not necessitate a visit from the social services, based on your absence… it is quite common that men of your age come home after a long teacake session, to find that their vulnerable wives have run off with the local orthopedic gym instructor.

Further to your enquiries whether there is a doppelgänger group of musicians called Brixton 9… certainly hope so.

And furthermore, your reference to Prontaprint and the relevant sizes of paper being A1, A2, A3 or A4… I suggest if you still have the use of your mobility scooter, let's keep it that way… we suggest maybe not waking up and getting yourself a bun, but making sure that your cupboards are stocked with fresh porridge oats, in which you'll find fibre, and which will keep you and your long suffering wife regular.

Love, *Larry Love*

PS Have you got any contact in Dignitas, where we can maybe work out a group discount?

Dear The Inspiral Carpets,

Re: Dragging Me Down

Within the above 'baggy smash' you state that you would search the world for me even though I can't imagine, add that you want to take me to China and, alarmingly, kiss me in Rome, and state that you would use rocket ships, mine sweepers and transistor radio receivers.

I write as a matter of extreme urgency, plasma rugs, and must insist that you fight any irresistible force and abort your foolhardy and no doubt highly expensive mission, which, contrary to your claim, I *am* capable of envisaging, forthwith.

I am not sure 'How It Should Be' that you have secured funding for this proposed expedition to me, celestial mattings, which sounds both extremely costly and convoluted, but can assure you that a lot of money can be saved in circumnavigating the earth in your me quest by my disclosure to you that I reside in Bournemouth.

This revelation, stellar druggets, should hopefully alleviate the necessity to deploy expensive spaceships, naval war vessels and wireless transmissions to establish my position. Indeed, celestial textile coverings, irrespective of my current whereabouts, I hope you will forgive my observing that your mode of exploratory transport is probably not the most expedient given that rockets are best renowned for travelling in an upward trajectory *vertically* through and *not* horizontally or diagonally across the sky. As you are no doubt aware, galactic runners, Dorset is not located in the upper atmosphere, and, given that the distance between Oldham and my home is 260 miles in a north to south linear direction, I think you would be better off getting a coach. Arguably, astronomical loop piles, it is technically feasible that your projectile could remain in stationary orbit above the planet and wait for it to rotate several degrees before re-entry and descent, preferably close to the pier; however, were you to miscalculate the plummet even fractionally, your intended splashdown could conceivably occur on dry land, perhaps on The Pavilion or Harry Ramsden's, whereby your gratuitous desires to break every bone of everybody in sight may well be granted.

I will have no part in this, star surfacings, and to this end have just conducted some investigations on your behalf and have established that Megabus are today quoting the very reasonable fare from Shudehill Interchange to Bournemouth Train Station of £155.00 for five passengers. Upon your arrival, I suggest a light lunch at The Moon In The Square on Exeter Road, so that I may 'Find Out Why' you are pursuing me.

I am afraid, however, that I must decline your offer of an excursion to the Orient, and intense clinching amongst other unwarranted intimacies in Italy's state capital, on the basis that I am very happily married and cannot recall where I last had my passport.

Finally, as regards your preposterous allegation that I am dragging you down, binary tufted weaves, I can most confidently assure you that at no time have I ever attempted to wrestle you to the floor, as evidenced not only by the fact that we have, to the best of my knowledge, never met, but also on account of my ongoing sciatica which would render any ground level grappling endeavours extremely inadvisable (and, for that matter, possibly futile, given your Farfisa organ player's solo assertion that 'you can't keep a good man down').

If you are agreeable to this compromise, I would be pleased to make the necessary arrangements in order that your loneliness may be curtailed.

Yours,

Derek Philpott

PS My wife Jean has just remarked from the kitchen (where she is making rock cakes) that our recent prize of a Dirty Harry box set at The Pokesdown & Southbourne Ex-Servicemen's Club raffle really was a 'Clint Boon'!

Dear Derek,

I feel drawn to reply to your missive. Although I am no longer with the fore said Inspiral Carpets, I did write the words to which you are reacting and can inform you that:

a) I am currently on the docks in Portsmouth awaiting a carriage to the IOW, so the stellar distances to which you are referring are not necessary at present, and

b) to inform you that the words were inspired by the idea of the United States' love of Saddam Hussein during the first Gulf War and weren't directly routed to you, although I thoroughly enjoyed the reading.

www.tomhingley.co.uk

....

Dear Derek,

Many thanks for your recent letter of concern. We hope this reply finds you well and also goes some way to putting you and your wife's minds at ease. We feel there has been a grave misunderstanding here and one, no matter how sensitive to some the subject matter may be, we will clarify shortly.

As you already know, we are now 5 hardy blokes from the North of England and are used to undertaking similar missions of 'derring do' despite the costs to us financially and physically.

We have already entered into the realms of space on that well known ship Saturn 5 and are currently undertaking a mission in that most iconic of WW2 fighter planes, the Spitfire. So, no matter how perilous and foolhardy these missions may seem, fear not. We will go to any lengths to please and excite our most loyal audience.

However, now to clarify the obvious misunderstanding expressed within your letter and put your mind at ease that you are safe and sound in Bournemouth. You may have heard that certain folk 'int' North share a bestial pastime and a love for a certain wool-encased animal. Therefore, when we state 'I will search this world for ewe, even though you can't imagine', we refer to both the love of this pastime, as well as the horror it causes outside of our boundaries.

Can you now see where the confusion lies and also why we have, until now, refrained from discussing this issue?

So, sleep safe and sound in your bed at night, Derek, with Jean, in the knowledge that we are not hunting you down. However, if you hear the fizz of a rocket or plane overhead and then the plaintive cry of a sheep nearby, don't look!

Yours,

The Inspiral Carpets

Dear Cornershop,
Against my better judgement, I decided to take your advice this afternoon when Jean and I took a post-casserole nap. The ill-advised manoeuvre led to my wife waking from a fitful sleep with a stiff back and mild respiratory problems.

Dear Roachford,
If, as you disturbingly state, you derive bliss exclusively from a synthetic stuffed animal, then you are quite right, Mr Roachford, I do 'feel for you', but only in the sense that I strongly recommend that you seek counselling immediately. For the love of God, man, for the love of God, stay out of Toys "R" Us!

Dear Flowered Up,

Re: 'Take it from me, I see what you don't see, I don't come down.'

I fully understand your impartation, my flora-raising chums, and have no reason to question your sincerity. It should be plainly apparent to anyone with even the remotest grasp of scale, altitude and perspective that the panorama to be enjoyed by one situated at a site of elevation is highly likely to be more extensive than that viewed at a lower vantage point. It remains unclear at the time of writing, however, just what you want me to relieve you of, or 'take from you', and how this may be achieved when allowing for gravitational aspects and vertical distance between us.

'It's On' a purely personal note that I must also express concern at your staunch refusal to descend, even for a 'comfort break' or a snack, and my wife Jean was wondering if there was any way that you could be presented with one of her homemade brownies and a bucket by the Fire Brigade, or possibly Bono, whom we understand to have climbed the highest mountain and therefore must be up to the errand on humanitarian grounds.

As regards your assertion that we will all be singing your tune, the less said the better, Flowered Up; you obviously have never heard me on the karaoke, which is enough to give anyone 'Philpott Phobia'!

Yours,

Derek Philpott

Dear Derek,

As one of the surviving ex-members of the beat combo known as Flowered Up, I feel it falls to me to reply to your correspondence as the perpetrator of the aforementioned lyric is no longer of this shire or, for that matter, this planet.

It's not strange you should note these particular lines from this song, as the verses were all written by a certain Joe Strummer and were purloined from the moving picture Rude Boy, and certainly carry more weight and sense than the chorus you refer to.

I regret to inform you I have no idea what Liam wished taken from him, perhaps a pair of X-ray glasses from the classified section of Viz he mistakenly believed gave him the power to visually undress women that failed to deliver on their promise; though this would explain the 'I see what you don't see' reference.

As for the refusal to come down, I believe this to be a blatant reference to the use of mildly psychedelic drugs that at some time in his past had permanently altered the chemical balance within his brain. He did eventually return to earth, but was ultimately disappointed.

As for the most gracious offer of some of Jean's famous brownies, we'd gladly be tempted by the unctuous delights anytime, preferably not delivered by Mr Bonio as he is obviously too busy avoiding tax and saving the planet. We would hate to distract him from these tasks. As for your karaoke rendition of Phobia, I shall reserve judgement until we are all ensconced in the snug of the Wasp and Griffin public house.

I bid you good day, sir.

I hope this clears up any misunderstanding and remain

Your servant,

Tim Dorney

Dear The Korgis,

We are just settling into a new home, my near-preferred monarchical domestic pet-monickered friends, and 'It Won't Be The Same Old Place' until 'The Way I Feel' is a lot warmer.

There were several 'Burning Questions' raised on our Homebuyer's Report, The Korgis, mainly concentrating on the inadequacy of the central heating system. However, together with my wife Jean, yours truly was so determined that 'I'll Be Here' by Easter that we foolhardily disregarded our solicitor's advice over a 'Cold Tea' to demand a reduction in the purchase price to reflect said neglected aquastat, substandard ventilation and sticky switch.

'That Was My Big Mistake', my misspelt, stumpy-legged, canine-homaging pals, for immediately upon moving in, the boiler conked out completely. To make matters worse, and spurred on by your advice on Magic FM at the time, I decided to try and save on mounting moving costs (having been brought up on rationing, 'I Just Can't Help It') and install a new one myself, rather than engage the services of a qualified CORGI (as in officially industry recognised as opposed to Royal dog overseen) engineer.

Needless to say, The Korgis, and with no such expert professional to 'Work Together' with and 'Show Me' where my stopcock was after my 'Third Time Around' the exterior of the property, and finding there was 'Nowhere To Run' the flue through without the appropriate heavy duty tools, I was forced to resort to a reputable local contractor to undertake the work properly.

It was only whilst watching Danny 'The Pipes, The Pipes Are Cooling' Boyle's dexterity in the near 'Silent Running' of his copper tube fitting and unit mounting today that I realised the glib perfunctoriness of your tenet 'Everybody's Got To Learn Sometime'. It was patently obvious from the intricacy and deftness of his work that young Daniel's skills were beyond those of a mere layperson and could not be mastered periodically at an indeterminate point. Indeed, it could even be argued that the craftsman might have been latently or genetically predisposed to his vocation and descended from a long line of plumbing specialists.

Ergo, to employ a similar principle, one finds it extremely doubtful that Mr Boyle would be so adept at performing successful cardiac transplants or, for that matter, whether pioneering surgeon Dr Christiaan Barnard would be so competent at installing a Worcester Greenstar 241 Compact Combi in our airing cupboard.

It is for this reason, The Korgis, and coming as I do from a printing background, that I must decline your credo to study so as to change my heart, whether it be via an adjustment to my existing one or a full replacement. I can further assure you that even were I to attempt such an operation (and its success, I agree would 'astound me'), I would most certainly not 'look around me' but instead be concentrating all efforts towards my thoracic cavity.

I further regret to inform you that your need for 'my loving' akin to solar radiance must remain unrequited for I have been happily married to my wife Jean for many years. That said, I am quite confident that your somewhat more restrained enquiry 'Can't We Be Friends Now?' could possibly be responded to in the affirmative, commencing perhaps with a small snack at an 'Intimate' eaterie equidistant to the both of us. I would ask that you are not tardy once a time has been agreed upon as there is little I abhor more than being kept in silent abeyance. No one likes to be one of the 'Dumb Waiters'!

I look forward to hearing from you.

Yours in anticipation,

Derek Philpott

Dear Sir,

We (The Korgis) would like to thank you for your letter. We are sorry to hear of your plumbing problems and do hope that they were resolved with the help of Mr Boyle. Frankly we are surprised that he is still plying his trade, what with the success of his mother Susan as a 'singing sensation'. Perhaps he has not experienced 'trickle down economics'.

As no doubt you are aware, we (that is James Warren and Andrew Cresswell Davis aka The Korgis) have been very busy over the last 45 years with our 'other band' – Stackridge. With that in mind we should point out that contrary to your assumption that we needed your loving, all we asked for was your 'Friendliness'. Indeed, we suggest that it would be a 'Victory For Common Sense' if you were to avoid any kind of 'Extravaganza' at a suitable hostelry, possibly choosing an establishment where the proprietor was 'The Man In The Bowler Hat'. As long as 'Dangerous Bacon' was not on the menu, we are confident that meeting with you for a small snack as you suggest would be most enjoyable. We leave it up to you to decide where, although '32 West Mall' might be a good choice as they do have a chap playing a 'Grande Piano'. As to when… how about 'Teatime'?

We (that is James Warren and Andrew Cresswell Davis aka The Korgis aka Stackridge) remain

'Fundamentally Yours'

Dear Mr. Jovi,
If, as you state, it doesn't make a difference whether 'Tommy' and 'Gina' make it or not, please could you clarify the importance of her taking his hand in order that they may achieve this irrelevant objective.

. . .

Dear Pete Townshend,
I think that My Generation is a very good 'pop song'. I impart this soundbite upon reading recently that you are fond of feedback.

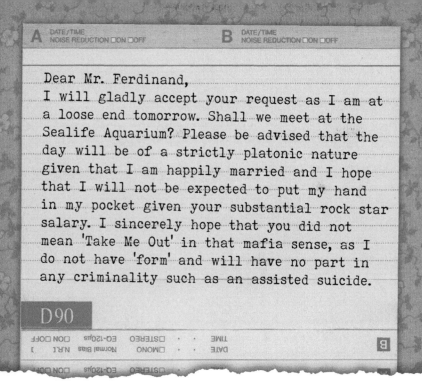

A DATE/TIME
NOISE REDUCTION ☐ON ☐OFF

B DATE/TIME
NOISE REDUCTION ☐ON ☐OFF

Dear Mr. Ferdinand,
I will gladly accept your request as I am at
a loose end tomorrow. Shall we meet at the
Sealife Aquarium? Please be advised that the
day will be of a strictly platonic nature
given that I am happily married and I hope
that I will not be expected to put my hand
in my pocket given your substantial rock star
salary. I sincerely hope that you did not
mean 'Take Me Out' in that mafia sense, as I
do not have 'form' and will have no part in
any criminality such as an assisted suicide.

D90

Dear Black Grape,

Re: Kelly's Heroes

I was recently dragged along (almost literally, I have ongoing sciatica) by some younger friends to the Queen's Park Hotel on Holdenhurst Road for the 'karaoke night' and was subjected to, amongst many other renditions, a particularly excruciating 'version' of one of my favourite Billy Joel songs by a burly man in tracksuit bottoms and a Prodigy T-shirt.

As it transpired, young Mike, with whom I enjoyed a medium Merlot afterwards, partly constructed from your band name, worked for the emergency services and was, in his own words, 'one of Dorset's premier house extinguishers and kitten/tree problem solvers', rendering his 'Firestarter' torso emblazonment and off-kilter 'We Didn't Start The Fire' rendition paradox to be in actuality most amusing.

I mention this incident, my darkened berry friends, merely because, despite your request that I 'don't talk to you about heroes' I feel that I must, specifically with reference to your implied disdain in suggesting that most of these men sing like serfs.

I am not ashamed to assure you of this, my ebony pre-raisin pals.

Were I to be in a burning building (such as my own) and Mike, or indeed any of his courageous colleagues, were to attend with a view to extracting me from said bungalow blaze, I, for one, would not refuse them a likely axe-wielded entry into my conflagrant premises upon the grounds of their inadequate vocal abilities being reminiscent of a feudal-system-restrained agricultural labourer. Furthermore, Black Grape, I fail to fathom how a perceived class strata may be able to determine one's ability to be endowed with the gift of competent chantability at the point of birth.

One is confident that this confusion is shared by David Essex, Joe Longthorne, and their dedicated followers.

Also, although both were men of principle who grew up without brothers or sisters, devoid of the physical support of both parents, and became intent on righting wrongs whilst garnering strong support, I was alarmed but then relieved to hear you blaspheme but then almost immediately retract your irreverent impiety that Jesus was Batman.

Finally, my ebony-fruit amigos, and in answer to your rather fervid enquiry as to who has the biggest, the biggest brain, luckily this came up at the Quiz Night at The Commodore on Overcliff Road last week. It is that of the sperm whale, which weighs in at around 8 kilograms, followed by the elephant and then the bottlenose dolphin.

I hope that I have been of assistance.

Yours,

Derek Philpott

PS Although on the whole one agrees that it is great to be straight ('yeah') I am not entirely sure that my friend Nigel Saxtonhouse would entirely concur with this philosophy at the moment. He has been very 'Stupid Stupid Stupid' and not had his Astra serviced for three years, and the steering column went just as he approached the Boundary Lane roundabout last week…

....

Dear Mr Philpott,

With regard to your recent enquiry as to the reason we obsidian berried chums hold such disdain for heroes, I refer you back to the original compact disc where we state (quite vigorously, I might add) 'DON'T TALK TO ME ABOUT HEROES'.

To receive your letter, which totally disregards our wishes, Mr Philpott, sir, having forked out at great cost (I might add) to procure the use of a fully equipped recording suite and a Herculean effort (and yes, the irony of the term Herculean is not lost to us) to attend said studio by myself and Mr Ryder, we vehemently declare at 32 hertz that we DO NOT condone heroics in any way, shape or form.

To read your correspondence, I have to admit, is very upsetting.

Having already received a cease and desist order from the Vatican with regard to our implying that the Papacy had helped members of the Nazi party evade incarceration at the end of the second world war, my esteemed colleague Mr Ryder and I were quite taken aback that you have chosen to zero in on the fact that we have stated that

'Jesus was a black man—No, Jesus was Batman!'

This will only be seen as a direct goading of the Catholic Church. Mr Ryder and I have neither the stomach nor the funds for another lengthy legal battle as we have considerable monetary obligations (e.g. hookers and drugs).

Mr Philpott, as a fellow human being and lover of cake, it is with a heavy heart that I ask you to please consider all the ramifications of your correspondence.

Yours *Kermit Leveridge*

Dear The Christians,

Re: Ideal World

Whilst 'flicking through' my new Freeview 'box' today I happened upon Channel 22 quite by chance and quite obviously felt impelled to write to you.

The Christians, I am absolutely humbled. If pop music's thus far brief history has taught us anything, it is surely that those of its proponents that lay claim to be able to soothsay (most notably Zager And Evans, Prince, and Busted) have been haplessly inept in comparison to your good selves, whose unimpeachably fastidious clairvoyance, released to the predominantly non-prognosticating 'record buying public' in December 1987, sagely foresaw the first transmission of one of QVC's closest rivals (launched on 17th April 2000) by a harbinger sceptic-silencing period of 13 years. In indisputable fact, not only was the tel-evisual retail emporium itself but also many of its key characteristics uncannily foretold by the highly melodic augury.

As you correctly heralded, all spectators are now indeed 'free to choose' from a multitude of never-to-be-repeated discounted bargains, rang-ing from, for example, stylish Raquel Welch wigs (hewn from fine, synthetic fibres) and the Snore Wizard, all the way through to the ultimate waterless car-cleaning product, and Steve Whatley's tan accel-erator, 'Zhuzh'. And, when an untimetabled blaze swept through the vending channel's Peterborough studio on 6th March 2001, a sudden blackout *did* stop the show and the whole thing *did* disappear, as also eerily and soulfully prophesied.

Although Ideal World does not have a 'catch-up option' (presumably owing to stock and pricing issues), your veracious divinations continue with firstly a direct reference to a handy feature on their website where 'we can start again' by reviewing all products featured in the previous hour's schedule, and secondly a recent episode at Philpott Place, whereupon my wife Jean recklessly purchased a 'Bricky Pro', 'Cricut' and 'Vergari Magnetic Knee Support' (all in the same month), at a total cost of £418.98; although this financial blow was softened by the utilisation of their 'Flexi-Basket', which enabled me to stagger the cost into three more manageable instalments, I had to tighten my belt for some weeks as 'my money filled their pockets', which led to some terse words in the household.

In recognition of your prodigious precognitive talents, one is tempted to suggest that you hawk your potential services to Psychic Today (Sky Channel 886), given that with calls to all sibyls charged at £1.53 per minute (plus network extras), the additional income could be a welcome augmentation to your existing pop star salaries. Sadly, however, this entrepreneurial advice is errant on two levels; your trading name may prove controversial and result in a slump in ratings considering its monotheistic connotations would be in direct conflict with the esoteric theme of your prospective employer; and I also think you will find it problematic – as portended in your song Hooverville – convincing even the most open-minded patrons of an imminent town built entirely from vacuum cleaners.

Jean and I therefore wish you continued success in your sole occupation as 'recording and touring artists'.

Amen to that!

Yours sincerely,

Derek Philpott

Hi Derek… sorry for delay in replying… been a bit crazy… new album out, gigs, promo here at Priestman Towers in the last 2 weeks… it's all go! Busy writing and gigging for next few days (and I need to give it serious thought!)… but I'm back home on Sunday, so will put my mind to it then. Feel free to nudge me on this email if you've not heard from me by next Wed.

… It's in the pipeline, Derek… I've got co-writer Mark Herman involved too (we wrote Ideal World together back in 1986). It's on our list 'to do'… thing is we're both Hull City fans, so it's a case of trying to get a song sorted by end of this week (as they're in FA Cup final). What exciting lives we lead :-)

… Hi Derek… spent a 3 hour journey to London (no distractions) trying to come up with something… Kept binning it… this is the hardest thing I've had to do since English A level I reckon (which I failed)!!… as it's there for all time, and for all to see (unlike my English A level), and what other people have written is great… (and yet I'm fine doing my pithy one liners on Facebook every day!)

… Hi Derek… So if you'll remain calm, and give us just a bit more leeway… then after that, if we don't manage it you can give us up as a dead loss, and tell us to finally p*** off!

Henry Priestman

....

I would never be so vulgar… Sling your hook!

Derek Philpott

ACKNOWLEDGEMENTS

Without the generosity, vision and support of the following people who backed this project, this book would not exist:

Aaron Miller
Adam Glover
Adrian Evans
Adrian Woodhouse
Adrienne White
Ariel Kaminsky
Aggie Sprung
Ailsa Townley
Ailsa Diamond
Ailsa McKillop
Alan Bambrough (plus Anna, Darayus and Rak)
Alan Toms
Alastair Bain
Alex Burton-Keeble
Alex Christie
Alex Lowrie
Alex Morris
Ali James
Alison Marrs
Alison Millar
Alison Millett
Allyson Miller
Amanda and Rob Austin
Amanda Gray
Amanda Patrie
Amy Volchok
Andi Bridges
Andre Luth
Andrew Forcer
Andrew Humeniuk
Andrew Long
Andrew Prestidge
Andrew Price
Andy Roberts
Andy Shardlow
Andy Kynaston
Andy Lumbard

Andy Macnaughton-Jones
Andy Phippen
Andy Spragg
Andy Thompson
Andy Tingey
Andy Wyatt
Angela Loughran
Angela Moore
Angela Varley
Angelika Ewald
Anita Park
Ann Maria Sutherland
Ann-Marie Van De Ven
Anna Harte
Anne Marie McGregor
Anthea Hawdon
Anthony Bromfield
Anthony McQuaid
Anthony Nash
Antony Pacitti
Arlene Wszalek
Arnie Medel
Arron Storey
Badger O'Donovan, dedicated to Ruby Elizabeth Henehan O'Donovan
Barbara Barry
Baz McAlister
Bee O'Wulf
Ben Richardson
Ben Wray
Benjamin Gott
Bernadette Stretch
Beth Allgood
Bev Punk Brock Tait
Bill Rusling
Bill Tasker
Billy Davidson

Blythe Duff
Bob Grover
Boz Mugabe
Bradley Martin
Brian De-Vine
Brian Grogan
Brian McCloskey
Brian Ormandy
Bridget Giles
Bryan Mackay
Carol Craven
Caleb O'Farrell Kreutlein
Caroline Mathews
Catherine Northing
Cathy Bishop
Celie Byrne
Charles Farrell
Charles Gladstone
Charlotte Riggio
Chris Bough
Chris Broughton
Chris Groom
Chris Nash
Chris Payne
Chris Sell
Chris Topham
Chrissie Pepper
Christiane Wenzl
Christine Coalter
Christopher Spalding
Christopher Wilson
Claire Bradley
Claire Farrell
Claire Mendelsohn
Clare Doody
Clare Kelly
Clare Lloyd
Clare Robinson

Claude Wolf
Cliff Moz Morris
Colin Sinclair
Colin Ursus-Thanatoid
Colleen Allen
Corey Moore
Craig Hilton
Craig Moss
Curig Jervis
Curt Smith
Cyan Jugo
Cyrillynn Chen
Dale Leopold
Damian O'Neill
Damon Parker
Dan Harrison
Dan Tutten
Dana Collins
Daniel Higgins
Daniel Varley
Daniele Mills
Danila Olmi
Darren Ramsay
Darren Riley
Dave Black
Dave Irving
Dave Stainer
Dave Whyman
David Paton
David Styles
David Barney
David Bascombe
David Baxter
David Boothman
David Carrier
David Dew
David Goody
David Griffiths
David Nicholson
David Norman
David Rachau
David Taylor
David Whitmore
Dawn Thorpe
Deb Talbot
Debbie Davies
Debbie Ghant
Debbie Thorne
Debbie Willetts
Deborah Jane Hegan

Debz Love Lewis
Dee Snelling
Denise Adamson
Derek Caney
Derek Philip
Derek Scott
Devi Cavaliere
Dewi Llwyd Evans
Diane Cockerham
Diane Hadfield
Diane Taylor
Dilwyn and Sandra Jones
Dirk Ewald
Margaret Ingham
Dom Richardson
Dominic Rodgers
Doug E Harper
Doug English
Douglas Milne
Douglas Young
Duncan Mawson
Duncan Parsons
Earl Grey Junior
Ed Smith
Ed Totten
Eddie Bawden
Eddiebaby
Effie Rubinstein
Ellie Skinner
Elizabeth Graham-Metz
Emiel Ramakers
Emily M Hetzel
Emily Walters
Emma Chetwynd Jarvis
Emmett Elvin
Erik James
Erik Rågvik
Estelle Rourke
Fan of the Lion and Unicorn,
    Maurice Thomas
Faye Carr
Fiona Karimjee
Fiona Knox
Fiona Macpherson
Fionnuala Dainty
Florent Die
Frances Mason
Frances McCabe
Francesca Lord
'Frankie from Germany'

Frank Whitney
Fred Fairbrass
Gary Bee
Gary Jefferies
Gary Mccrindle
Gary Sadler
Gary Sanders
Gary Shaw
Gary Woodbridge
Gavin Hallesy
Gaynor Clarkson
Ged Hayes
Geoff Richardson
Georgia McGrane
Gergely Szalay
Gertie Grocott
Gertrude Lok
Giles Chesher
Gill McGregor
Gillian Coe
Glen De La Cour
Graeme Houston
Graham Burbage
Graham Mckay-Smith
Gregory Anderson
Guy Moore
Hanneke Joustra
Heather Allen
Helen Bound
Helen Bristow
Helen Brown
Helen Leighs Smith
Helen Morris
Helen Roughley
Helen Stephens
Helen Vickers
Henri Weterings
Henrietta Penn
Henry Priestman
Hollie Moore
Hugh Edwards
Hugh Jones
Iain Freeman
Iain MacInnes
Ian Aghakhanieyan
Ian Baguley
Ian Chennell
Ian French
Ian James
Ian Jones

Ian Kucera-Skinner
Ian McKay
Ian O'Beirne
Ian Ellison-Taylor
Ingo Molin
Innes Morrison
Iona Houston
J. Pattingale
Jack Fleming
Jack Healy
Jackie Winn
Jain Reid
Jaine Henderson
Jakob Lundqvist
James Aylett
James Clarke
James Park
James Shardlow
Jamie Jones
Jamie O'Brien Moore
Jan Robinson
Jane Absolom
Jane Antoinette Croucher
Jane DelFavero
Jane Hoe
Jane Trobridge
Janet Gow
Janine Ramsey
Jason Neville
Jason Read
Janine F Luff Davies
Jeanne Smith
Jeannie Lack
Jeff Cooper
Jeff Lenton
Jeff Parry
Jenni Lawson
Jenny Ashcroft
Jeremy Smith
Jez Scott
Jill Bloomfield
Jim Finnis
Jim Hamilton
Jim Hamshaw
Jo Ann Enk
Jo Gannon
Jo Higgins
Jo Parker
Joan Mason
Joanna Cummings

Jodi Irwin
Joel DL Baass
John Clay
John Glover
John and Judith Ireland
John Howard Jones
John Mcloughlin
John Noble
John Quinn
John Robert Allen
John (Vernham Chronicles)
  Saunders
John Smith
John K Smith
John and Sharon Schofield
John Scott
John Smith
John Willcox
Jon Pollard
Jon Shaw
Jon Stretch
Jon Western
Jon Yard
Jonathan Birkett
Jonathan Guard
Jonathan Whiteside
Jordan Reyne
Joseph Cairns
Juan Christian
Judith Barrow
Judith Parry
Judy Groom
Jules Dawes
Julian Benfield
Julian Maddison
Julianne Regan
Julie Harford
Julie Hemmings
Julie Taylor
Justin Brice
Justine 'Dusty' Levett
Justine Roddick
Karen Wehrle
Karn West
Karol Cooper
Kasia 'Depends' Baczkowski
Kate Croucher
Kate Sheppard
Kate Simpson
Kath Bull

Kath McCarron
Kathi Kolb
Katia Kreutlein
Katinka Van der Harst
Katy Purvis
Kaz Price
Keith Andrews
Keith Bell
Keith Watterson
Kel Barrass
Ken Worthing
Kerry Gregory
Kerry Hodson
Kerry Wang
Kevin and Elaine Davis
Kevin E. Knapp
Kevin Moore
Kevin Shults
Kevin Thompson
Kieron Neaves
Kim Halliday
Kim McCann Henry
Kimberly Rogers
Kirsten Hegarty
Knut Berg
Kris Tarplee
Kristina Schlegel
Lesley Brothwood
Lana Dragicevich
Lance Dawkins
Laura Brightman
Laura Catchpole
Laura Warburton
Lee Griffiths
Leigh Allen
Leigh Valens
Lennaert Roomer
Leon Clowes
Lesley O'Hara
Liam O'Hare
Lindsey Robinson
Lisa Arnott
Lisa Brown
Lisa Davies
Lisa Eaden
Lisa Gironda
Lisa Hunt
Lisa Ann Sworn
Lisa Turner
Liz Kentish

Logan Murray
Lorna Hughes
Lorny Dune
Lorri Cumming
Louise Doherty
Lucy Isles
Luis Vallespín
Lynn Howarth
Lynn Lewis
Lynn Johnston
Lynn Wyeth
Lynne Baldham
Lynne Smith
Lynton Cox
Mac McFadden
Mandy Kenyon
Mare Rozzelle
Marianne Walker
Marie Brett
Marie Corr
Mariko Nobukuni
Mark Chadderton
Mark Cottrell
Mark Gallacher
Mark Grant
Mark Hyde
Mark Lew Lewis
Mark Lingard
Mark McClymont
Martin Bullard
Martin Coogan
Martin McCann
Martin Read
Mary Reese
Mat Hammond
Mary Hillier Redmond
Matt Thorne
Matthew McEvoy
Matthew Schiavello
Maurice Wilkie
Max Crowe
Maxine Jones
Maxine Ogara
Meg Sussman
Mel Maidment
Melinda Kelly
Melissa-Jayne Widger
Michael Tich Anderson
Michael Bourne
Michael Day

Michael Legge
Michael Murphy
Michelle Knight
Michelle O'Connor
Anitra Novy (Mighty Ani)
Mike Barrett
Mike Harman
Mike Smith
Ian 'Mobs' Mobley
Mrs Scorbie and The Scorbies
Naomi Williams
Natalie Barwell
Natalie Rudley
Neil Babbage
Neil Carney
Neil Hughes
Neil McGregor
Neil Roberts
Neil Skinner
Neil Spragg
Neil Warburton
Neil White
Nick Bourne
Nick Hale
Nick Hardy
Nick Loebner
Nicky Young
Nigel Frost
Nigel Karl Stone
Nigel Proktor
Nora Gause
Olivia Fawkes
Onomatopoeia Records
Patrick Dalton
Paul Vanags
Paul Ashby
Paul Butler
Paul de Csernatony
Paul Findon
Paul Mancini
Paul Maskell
Paul McMahon
Paul and Patricia McKernan
Paul Newson
Paul Scott
Paul Shuff
Paul Watson
Paul Weaver
Peg Cizek
Penny Kirsner

Per-Christian Hille
Peta Bough
Peta Foley
Peta Lord
Pete Attard
Pete Dee
Pete Hughes
Pete R Jones
Peter and Rachel
Peter Beech
Peter Davis
Peter Edmunds
Peter Fitzpatrick
Peter Gifford
Peter Hallsworth
Peter McCormack
Peter Newbould
Peter O'Callaghan
Peter Ross
Peter Young
Phil Bonshor
Phil Brunnen
Phil Clifford
Phil Grant
Phil Oates
Phil Wild
Philippa Day
Rachael South
Rachel McCarthy
Rachel Padgett
Randy Wagner
Ralph Cade
Ralph Kreisl
Ralph White
Rebecca Harper
Rebecca Kershaw
Renee Rosen-Wakeford
Rhonda Baugh
Rich Davenport
Richard Callan
Richard Fairbrass
Richard Ponsford
Richard Stott
Richard Butchins
Ricky (Fred) Burchell
Rob Buckle
Rob Crawford
Rob Davis
Rob Howes
Rob Yuill

Robert Alfonso
Robert Rosendahl
Robert Sim
Robin Fransella
Rockula
Rod Tate
Roi Croasdale
Ron Faulkner
Rosie McLaughlin
Rosine Smyrl
Roy Corkill
Roy Long
Roy Smith
Ruby Pepper
Russ Pinney
Russell Tomlinson
Ruth Bertram
Ruth McQuinn
Ruth Patrak
Ruth Steele
Samantha Reynolds
Sandra Kowalczyk
Sarah Bromfield
Sarah Eaves
Sarah Fitzpatrick
Sarah Graham
Sarah Hasted
Sarah McDonnell
Sarah Naomi Brownrigg
Sarah Nightingale
Sarah O'Leary
Sarah Williamson
Sarah-Jane Moon
Sarah Farrell
Sarahjane Patterson
Sarah March-Paschal
Scot Mathieson
Scott Brownlow
Scott D Fay
Scott Hubbard
Shani Simpson
Sharon Lacey
Sharon Schofield
Sharon Wheeler
Sharron Hather
Shelley Warren
Simon Bottery
Simon Glinn

Simon Joiner
Simon Mulligan
Siobhan McClelland
Siobhan O'Brien
Spike Worsley
Stephen 'Goughy' Gough
Stefanie Bristow
Stefano Gilardino
Stephen Plott
Stephen Dewison
Stephen Edwards
Stephen Griffith
Stephen Hancock
Stephen 'Fluff' Roberts
Stephen Teixeira
Steve and Kerry Vincent
Steve Bell
Steve Birbeck
Steve Cobham
Steve Gibson
Steve Grose
Steve Hill
Steve Rauer (Fin
   Gersandthumbs)
Steve Roffey
Steve Walters
Steve Wells
Suzanne Hill
Steven Browne
Steven Dean
Stevo Feeney
Stewart Burns
Stewart Thompson
Stuart Adam
Stuart Benjamin
Sue Abson
Sue Brearley
Sue Deacon
Sue Morbi
Tanya Palmer
Tara O'Shea-Robinson
Tasmin Archer
Teresa Hayes
Thomas Newton
Tim Brooks
Tim and Kate Dorney
Tim Ellis
Tim Holmes

Tim James
Tim Quy
Tim Romain
Tim Russell
Tim Stevens
Tim Tearle
T.J. Johnson Howe
Tom Crossley
Tom Curtis
Tom De Geytere
Tom Enzerink
Tom Ford
Tom Gordon
Tom Moody-Stuart
Tom Seago
Tomas Bremin
Tony Hall
Tony Kearon
Tony Manley
Tony Quinn
Tony Paul Way
Tracey Hunt
Tracey MacKenzie
Traci-Ann DiSalvatore
Tracy Collins
Tyrianny Noyb
Vicki Cattermoul
Vicki Nanfito
Vicki Thompson
Vicky Walker
Viki Vortex
Vincent Ryan
Vincent Van Veen
Warren Lapworth
Wayne Owen
Wendy Brunt
Wendy Santori
Will Warburton
William Kelly
Willy Barden
Yazz
Yvonne Roberts
Yvonne Watterson
Zena Barrie
Zoe Dingwall
Zoe Watters

Bless the lot of you!

Very special thanks to the following for obtaining replies, and support:

Olivia Fawkes, Tim Quy, Patrick Dalton, Pete Dee, Keith Bell, Francesca Lord, Kev Moore, Dirk Ewald, Keith and Yvonne Watterson, Phil Bonsor, Pete R Jones, Jake Blight, Kim Halliday, Angela Cranwell, my friend Daniel Wylie (a criminally overlooked talent), Martin Coogan, Angela Loughran, Clive Leighton, Alan Roots, Steve 'Slim' Wainwright, Jim Rowland, Toby Woby, Colin UT Bear (who started it with first reply) and Lorna Willetts, Tim Brooks, Ged Hayes, Maurice Thomas, Bruce Dessau, Jacky Carroll, Brian Grogan, The Scorbies, The Patraks, Vic Godard and Georgie, Julianne Regan, Rachel McCarthy, Richard Butchins, Roy Corkill (an impossible task without you, you lovely man), Chris Topham (there are no words to express my thanks), Bruce Thomas (a like-minded thinker who I am humbled to call a friend), Tosh Flood, John Robert Allen, Vicki Cattermoul, Gary Jefferies, Frank Jordan, Lynton Cox and Martin Shuttlecock from Café Spike, Tom Denton, Spike Worsley, Peter Broughton-Rates, Ged Hayes, Graham and all at Viz (you lovely people), John Roberts, David 'Gibby' Gibson, Buttz BabyIdol, Dave Bascombe, Jackie Winn, Johnny 'debonair' Debonair, Richard Ponsford, Sharon Lacey, Peter Lee Smith, Neil Hughes, Neil Warburton, Clare Bown, Alan Cooke, Jules Scott, Pippa Reid, Nigel Karl Stone, Dee Snelling, Lisa Eaden, Tom and Sue (tomrobinson.com 'Only The Now'), Steve Hancock, Jamie Kynaston, Andy Kynaston, Dougie Milne, Ty Atkins, Mark Gallacher, Mike Smith, Steve Kifaru, Daz Walters, Amanda Austin, Kavus Torabi, Pete Dee, and James Marett at www.oastone. co.uk (without whom the book and website would not exist).

Lastly, I would very much like to thank my son, David, not only for introducing me to such varied music, but for making these letters a textual reality. He has taken my words, comments and questions, and transformed them with cohesion and continuity into the printed form that you see today. He didn't want to be acknowledged, but I feel it's only right that he gets the recognition he deserves for all his patience and hard work, and for turning these shenanigans into a reality.

SONG CREDITS

With apologies and thanks to the authors of all song lyrics used, who are in no way to blame for the content of outgoing letters:

10cc, 'I'm Not In Love' © Schubert Music Publishing Ltd

ABC, 'When Smokey Sings' © BMG Rights Management US LLC/EMI Music Publishing/Sony/ATV Music Publishing LLC

Bryan Adams, 'Everything I Do (I Do It For You)' © Zachary Creek Music Inc., Miracle Creek Music Inc., Almo Music Corp., 2855 Music, Loon Echo Inc., Brian Adams Music

The Adverts, 'Gary Gilmore's Eyes' © Warner/Chappell Music, Inc.

Alabama 3, 'Woke Up This Morning' © Warner/Chappell Music, Inc., BMG Rights Management US LLC

All About Eve, 'Martha's Harbour' © Sony/ATV Music Publishing LLC/Emi Music Publishing Ltd

Anvil, 'Metal On Metal' © Peermusic Publishing

Tasmin Archer, 'Sleeping Satellite' © BMG Rights Management US LLC

Rick Astley, 'Never Gonna Give You Up' © Universal Music Publishing Group, Sony/ATV Music Publishing LLC

Baby Bird, 'You're Gorgeous' © Chrysalis Music Ltd/BMG Rights Management US LLC

Beck, 'Where It's At' © Universal Music Publishing Group

The Bee Gees, 'Stayin' Alive' © Sony/ATV Music Publishing LLC, Warner/Chappell Music, Inc., Universal Music Publishing Group

Beyonce, 'Irreplaceable' © Sony/ATV Music Publishing LLC, Warner/Chappell Music, Inc., Universal Music Publishing Group, Z Songs, EMI Music Publishing, B-Day Publishing, Super Saying Publishing, EMI April Music Inc, Stellar Songs Ltd

Black Grape, 'Kelly's Heroes' © OBO APRA/AMCOS

Black Sabbath, 'Paranoid' © TRO Inc.

Bon Jovi, 'Livin' On A Prayer' © Sony/ATV Music Publishing LLC, Universal Music Publishing Group, Aggressive Music, Bon Jovi Publishing

David Bowie, 'Ashes To Ashes' © EMI Music Publishing, Tintoretto Music

Billy Bragg, 'The Milkman Of Human Kindness' © Sony/ATV Music Publishing LLC/

Captain Sensible, 'Wot' © Universal Music Publishing Group, Anglo-Rock, Inc.

The Carpenters, 'Close To You' © Warner/Chappell Music, Inc., BMG Rights Management US LLC, Universal Music Publishing Group

Cher, 'If I Could Turn Back Time' © Universal Music Publishing Group, Realsongs

The Christians, 'Ideal World' © Sony/ATV Music Publishing LLC

The Clash, 'Should I Stay Or Should I Go?' © Universal Music Publishing Group

Colonel Abrams, 'Trapped' © Warner/Chappell Music, Inc., Universal Music Publishing Group

The Communards, 'Don't Leave Me This Way' © EMI Music Publishing, Sony/ATV Music Publishing LLC Warner/Chappell Music, Inc.,Universal Music Publishing Group,Warner-tamerlane Publishing Corp.

Culture Club, 'I'll Tumble 4 Ya' © EMI Music Publishing, BMG Rights Management US LLC, Sony/ATV Music Publishing LLC

Def Leppard, 'Pour Some Sugar On Me'
© BMG Rights Management US LLC

Alesha Dixon, 'The Boy Does Nothing'
© Sony/ATV Music Publishing (UK)
Limited, Warner/Chappell Music Ltd,
Xenomania Songs, MG Rights Management
US LLC

Elvis Costello And The Attractions, 'Oliver's
Army' © Universal Music Publishing Group

Crowded House, 'Weather With You' © BMG
Rights Management US LLC

Danny Wilson, 'Mary's Prayer' © Nettwerk 1
Music

R Dean Taylor, 'There's A Ghost In My House'
© Sony/ATV Music Publishing LLC

Del Amitri, 'Nothing Ever Happens'
© Polygram Music Publishing Ltd GB

Department S, 'Is Vic There?' © EMI Music
Publishing, Sony/ATV Music Publishing
LLC

The Divine Comedy, 'National Express'
© Universal Music Publishing Group, BMG
Rights Management US LLC

Sophie Ellis-Bextor, 'Murder On The
Dancefloor' © Universal Music Publishing
Group, BMG Rights Management US LLC

The Eurythmics, 'Who's That Girl?'
© Universal Music Publishing Group

Fish/Marillion, 'Sugar Mice' © Marillion
Music, Charisma Music Pub. USA, Inc.

Flowered Up, 'Take It' © Universal Music
Publishing Group/Notting Hill Music

Franz Ferdinand, 'Take Me Out' © Universal
Music Publishing Ltd

Free, 'All Right Now' © OBO APRA/
AMCOS, Blue Mountain Music Ltd, Cohen
& Cohen

Dean Friedman, 'Lydia' & others referenced
© Dean Friedman Music (PRS)

Fun Boy Three/The Gogos, 'Our Lips Are
Sealed' © Universal Music Publishing Group

Peter Gabriel, 'Sledgehammer' © Real World
Music Ltd, Fox Film Music Corp. OBO
Fourteen Ninety Two Music, Universal
Music, Careers

Genesis, 'Follow You Follow Me' © EMI
Music Publishing, Imagem US LLC

Go West, 'Don't Look Down' © Sony/ATV
Music Publishing LLC/Universal Music
Publishing Group/Warner/Chappell Music,
Inc.

Vic Godard & Subway Sect, with kind
permission from V Godard for all titles &
lyrics used

Gonzalez, 'I Haven't Stopped Dancing Yet'
© Universal Music Publishing Group

Steve Harley & Cockney Rebel, 'Make Me
Smile (Come Up And See Me)' © OBO
APRA/AMCOS, Music & Media Int'l, Inc.

Haysi Fantayzee, 'John Wayne Is Big Leggy'
© Carbert Music Inc., Chrysalis Music Ltd

Chesney Hawkes, 'The One And Only'
© Copyright: Imagem Songs Ltd, Chrysalis
Songs

Heaven 17, All titles © Sony/ATV Music
Publishing LLC, Warner/Chappell Music,
Inc., BMG Rights Management US LLC,
© Kobalt Music Publishing Ltd, Universal
Music Publishing Group,, Royalty Network

Hue & Cry, 'Labour Of Love' © Warner/
Chappell Music, Inc., Kobalt Music
Publishing Ltd, Universal Music Publishing
Group

The Human League, 'Mirror Man'/'Don't You
Want Me' © Universal Music Publishing
Group/BMG Rights Management US LLC/
EMI Music Publishing/Sony/ATV Music
Publishing LLC

The Icicle Works, 'Love Is A Wonderful
Colour' © Peermusic Publishing

Inspiral Carpets, 'Dragging Me Down'
© Universal Music Publishing Group, BMG
Rights Management US LLC

It's Immaterial, 'Driving Away From Home
(Jim's Tune)' © BMG Rights Management
US LLC, Rosetta Vm Pka Virgin Music
Lyrics

Janet Jackson, 'What Have You Done For Me
Lately?' © Sony/ATV Music Publishing LLC

Joe Jackson, 'Is She Really Going Out With
Him?' © Sony/ATV Music Publishing LLC

The Jacksons, 'Blame It On The Boogie'
© Chrysalis Music Holdings Gmbh, GEMA

The Jam, "A' Bomb In Wardour Street'
© Universal Music Publishing Group

Jethro Tull, 'Songs From The Wood' © The
Ian Anderson Group Of Companies Ltd,
BMG Rights Management US LLC

JoBoxers, 'Just Got Lucky'/'Boxerbeat' © Sony
Music Entertainment Publishing: Imagem/
Black Dream Music

Elton John, 'Candle In The Wind' © Universal Music Publishing Group

Howard Jones, 'Like To Get To Know You Well' © OBO APRA/AMCOS, Songs Of Kobalt Music Pub OBO Howard Jones Music America

Judas Priest, 'Exciter' © Sony/ATV Music Publishing LLC

Kajagoogooo, 'Too Shy' © Sony/ATV Music Publishing LLC

Nik Kershaw, 'Wouldn't It Be Good?' © Imagem Songs Ltd/Universal Music Publishing Group

The Killers, 'Human' © Universal Music Publishing Ltd

The Korgis, 'Everybody's Gotta Learn Sometimes' © Warner/Chappell Music, Inc.

Lady Gaga, 'Born This Way' © House Of Gaga Publishing LLC, Warner Tamerlane Publishing Corp., Sony/ATV Songs LLC, Universal Music Corp., Garibay Music Publishing, Glostream Music Publishing, Universal-polygram International Publishing Inc.

Level 42, 'Lessons In Love' © Universal Music Publishing Ltd

Jona Lewie, 'You'll Always Find Me In The Kitchen At Parties' © Universal Music Publishing Group

Living In A Box, 'Living in a Box' © Sony/ATV Music Publishing LLC

Madonna, 'Like A Prayer' © Emi Blackwood Music Inc., Orangejello Music, Crk Music Inc., Webo Girl Publishing Inc., Universal Music Publishing Ltd, Johnny Yuma Music, Associated Music International Ltd, WB Music Corp. Sire Records, WEA International, Bleu Disque Music Co.

All Mansun references © Universal Music Publishing Ltd, with permission granted by P Draper

Matt Bianco, 'Get Out Of Your Lazy Bed' © Warner/Chappell Music, Inc.

Ralph McTell, 'Streets Of London' © TRO Inc.

Mel & Kim, 'Showing Out' © Sony/ATV Music Publishing LLC/Universal Music Publishing Group/Mike Stock Publishing Limited, Sids Songs Ltd, All Boys Music Ltd

The Members, 'The Sound Of The Suburbs' © BMG Rights Management US LLC

The Mock Turtles, 'Can You Dig It?' © Sony/ATV Music Publishing LLC, BMG Rights Management US LLC

The Moody Blues, 'Nights In White Satin' © TRO Inc.

Motorhead, 'Ace Of Spades' © EMI Music Publishing, Sony/ATV Music Publishing LLC, Universal Music Publishing Group

Mr. Mister, 'Broken Wings' © Warner/Chappell Music, Inc., Panola Park Music, Hanseatic Musikverlag Gmbh & Co. Kg, Ali-aja Music, Indolent Sloth Music, WB Music Corp.

The Only Ones, 'Another Girl Another Planet' © P Perrett

Prince, 'Take Me With You' © WB Music Corp./Controversy Music/Warner Olive Music LLC, © Universal Music Publishing Group

The Piranhas, 'Tom Hark'/'Green Don't Suit Me', Kind Permission granted by Bob Grover

Public Image Limited, 'This Is Not A Love Song' © Sony/ATV Music Publishing LLC, Warner/Chappell Music, Inc., Universal Music Publishing Group, BMG Rights Management US LLC, EMI Music Publishing

REM, 'Stand' © Night Garden Music

Republica, 'Ready To Go' © Sony/ATV Music Publishing LLC, Warner/Chappell Music, Inc.

Right Said Fred, 'I'm Too Sexy' © Spirit Music Group

Roachford, 'Cuddy Toy' © Warner/Chappell Music, Inc., Universal Music Publishing Group

Tom Robinson, '2-4-6-8 Motorway' © Conexion Media Group, Inc.

Roxy Music, 'Dance Away' © Universal Music Publishing Group, EG Music Ltd

Sad Café, 'Everday Hurts' © Sony/ATV Music Publishing LLC/EMI Music Publishing

Sailor, 'A Glass Of Champagne' © Morris Music, Inc.

Steve Miller Band, 'Abracadabra' © Universal Music Publishing Group

Saxon, 'Wheels Of Steel' © Carlin America Inc.

Sigue Sigue Sputnik, 'Love Missile F1-11' © Universal Music Publishing Group

Simply Red, 'Stars' © EMI Music Publishing

Smokie, 'Mexican Girl'/'Oh Carol' © BMG Rights Management US LLC, Universal Music Publishing Group/Sony/ATV Music Publishing LLC

Space, 'Neighbourhood' © Sony/ATV Music Publishing LLC, Universal Music Publishing Group, Ultra Tunes

Spandau Ballet, 'Musclebound' © Reformation Publishing USA

Squeeze, 'Up The Junction' © Universal Music Publishing Group

The Specials, 'A Message To You Rudy' © Carbert Music Inc., Carlin Music Corp

Stereo MCs, 'Step It Up'/'Connected' © Sony/ATV Music Publishing LLC, BMG Rights Management US LLC

Stiff Little Fingers, 'Gotta Gettaway' © Sony/ATV Music Publishing LLC, Universal Music Publishing Group

The Stranglers, 'Straighten Out' © Universal Music Publishing Group, Albion Music Ltd,

The Sweet, 'Blockbuster' © EMI Music Publishing, Universal Music Publishing Group

Take That, 'Never Forget' © Sony/ATV Music Publishing LLC, BMG Rights Management US LLC, Universal Music Publishing Group

Talking Heads, 'Burning Down The House' © Warner/Chappell Music, Inc.

Technotronic, 'Pump Up The Jam' © Sony/ATV Music Publishing LLC, Universal Music Publishing Group, Bogam, BMC Publishing

Tears For Fears, 'Sowing The Seeds of Love' © BMG Vm Music Ltd

Thompson Twins, 'Doctor Doctor' © Universal Music Publishing Group

Toto Coelo, 'I Eat Cannibals' © Sony/ATV Music Publishing LLC/Sm Publishing UK Limited

Toyah, 'I Want To Be Free' © OBO APRA/AMCOS, EMI Music Publishing, Sweet 'N' Sour Songs Ltd

Tracy Chapman, 'Fast Car' © Sony/ATV Music Publishing LLC

Frank Turner, 'The Road' © Universal Music Publishing Group

Ultravox, 'Dancing With Tears In My Eyes' © Sony/ATV Music Publishing LLC, Universal Music Publishing Group

The Undertones, 'My Perfect Cousin' © Universal Music Publishing Group

Was (Not Was), 'Walk The Dinosaur' © Universal Music Publishing Group

The Who, 'My Generation' © TRO Inc.

Kim Wilde, 'Kids In America' © EMI Music Publishing/Rak Publishing Ltd

Stevie Wonder, 'Signed, Sealed Delivered I'm Yours' © EMI Music Publishing, Sony/ATV Music Publishing LLC

The Wurzels, 'Combine Harvester' © Sony/ATV Music Publishing LLC/OBO APRA/AMCOS, EMI Music Publishing

Yazz, 'The Only Way Is Up' © Peermusic Publishing, Universal Music Publishing Group

15227113R00134

Printed in Great Britain
by Amazon.co.uk, Ltd.,
Marston Gate.